THE GLORIOUS GROUSE

DAVID & CHARLES' FIELDSPORTS AND FISHING TITLES

Brian P. Martin

THE GLORIOUS GROUSE

A Natural and Unnatural History

**Foreword by His Grace
The Duke of Westminster**

DAVID & CHARLES
Newton Abbot   London

*To all those moorland owners and keepers who
provide such excellent sport and protect
Britain's uplands*

British Library Cataloguing in Publication Data

Martin, Brian P. (Brian Philip), 1947–
  The Glorious grouse.
  1. Livestock : Grouse
  I. Title
  636.59

ISBN 0-7153-9237-9

Typeset by Typesetters (Birmingham) Ltd, Smethwick, West Midlands
and printed in Great Britain
by The Bath Press
for David & Charles Publishers plc
Brunel House   Newton Abbot   Devon

Contents

Foreword

The Glorious Grouse is a fascinating work by an author who has a clear understanding and love of the countryside. Practical experience together with a sense of history are an unusual combination when books on this subject are written and the rich vein of these attributes permeate through his work.

The grouse is a perplexing and fascinating bird, maddeningly frustrating on occasions; however providing, as it does, the finest sport in the World in surroundings that are supreme. It is a bird that combines mystery and uniqueness and for those of us who are fortunate enough to either own or manage a moor, it is a continual challenge.

The author describes clearly the other benefits in terms of conservation of wildlife, flora and fauna and, as importantly, the preservation of the uplands that the managed moor brings to the quality of our countryside. For it is abundantly clear that the aims and objectives of the moor owner in terms of the preservation of heatherland and the grouse are inextricably linked.

The author combines a deep knowledge and a sense of fun in this book and I have no hesitation in commending it to you.

THE DUKE OF WESTMINSTER
Eaton Hall · Chester

Introduction

Most sportsmen fortunate enough to have hunted all British quarry have no hesitation in acknowledging the red grouse as 'King of Gamebirds'. Certainly almost all the many great-shoot owners I have met insist that grouse-shooting is the most glorious of sports. From big game in Africa to pigeon in the Home Counties, no quarry has fired these discerning men with so much excitement as the red grouse, and no environment has brought them the great joy to be found on the heather moorlands of upland Britain. The glorious red grouse is unique to these islands.

But no longer is grouse-shooting only for privileged autocrats. Today fatness of wallet is more important than impeccable pedigree and many 'outsiders' – including at least one Arab sheikh – have bought the sporting rights to important moors. And since the middle of the nineteenth century wealthy Americans have needed little prompting in buying our best let days – often much to the chagrin of outgunned locals. As one Californian told me recently, on his seventeenth consecutive annual visit to a leading Scottish moor, 'grouse-shooting is a disease which you can catch all too easily and they have yet to find a cure.'

Fortunately you do not have to be a millionaire to savour the glories of grouse: walked-up sport over pointers and setters can still be had for a few tens of pounds rather than the many hundreds necessary to secure a place in a distinguished line of butts. Every year men from all walks of life eagerly save their hard-earned pennies for one short sortie in grouseland. Of course they miss out on the smoked salmon and double-gun, 100-brace days, but at least they can share the stimulating countryside of this truly wild gamebird, with the purple mountains leading ever onward into glory.

Unlike the pheasant and partridge, the grouse is not the subject of widespread release schemes: it can be reared in captivity but does not adapt well to its natural diet – predominantly heather – when turned out. Thus grouse-men concentrate on habitat management and have bequeathed us this wonderful legacy of heather moorland – now home to a wide range of endangered animals and plants as well as the most exhilarating of landscapes in largely tamed Britain.

Because they are not hand reared, the grouse retain all their cunning, passing valuable gene pools from one generation to the next. They are also naturally strong and tremendously agile on the wing, a good driven bird providing one of the most testing of marks – quite the opposite of the pathetic picture of 'slaughter' commonly portrayed by the popular press.

Railway advertisement (1922)

Grouse are highly territorial birds which often display from prominent rocks. Painting by Archibald Thorburn (Courtesy of the Tryon Gallery)

As a sport, grouse-shooting is scarcely two centuries old, and over the last hundred years the 'muirfowl' has generated so much interest it could easily be buried in the mountain of literature already devoted to it. However, the great majority of these words have concentrated on the bird's value to Scotland's economy and the mysteries of population fluctuations. Indeed, the amount of research devoted to the red grouse is forever increasing, with many hundreds of thousands of words discussing grouse disease and over-grazing of moors alone.

Undoubtedly, improved scientific analysis is providing much valuable new information, to the benefit of the red grouse and the many other species which share its habitat, not to mention the shooters, of course. Yet the cyclical nature of grouse populations continues and it is not difficult to detect the wry smile of inevitability on the face of the long-established moor-owner when the subject of research is raised. Though not apathetic, many seem content with the uncertainty of each season, and reassured by their reliance on good, traditional keepering, the lack of which has been the undoing of many moors. Indeed, much of the magic would disappear if consistently high bags of this wild quarry could be more or less guaranteed, in the way of commercial pheasant-shooting.

Perhaps too much emphasis has been placed on the maintenance of bag levels because this sport of grouse-shooting has become largely a business, inextricably linked with the national economy. Obviously, the smaller the bags the lower the moor-owner's income. In the old days, when commercialism never entered into it, Guns went out much more often and were content with much smaller bags.

On the other hand, increasing interest in commercial shooting has many advantages. For example, it provides the stimulus to preserve a moor and develop its full potential, especially in these days when only a handful of the very richest men can afford to entertain in the old style. Neither is pursuit of large bags necessarily a bad thing for moorland conservation as the most successful moor managers have always included some whose maxim has been to shoot as hard as possible. Indeed, one of the most acclaimed in modern times always said 'shoot every grouse in sight'. The result has been a moor with exceptionally consistent high bags and very little disease. And rather surprisingly, the increased disturbance has done little to upset other wildlife: on the contrary, the populations of some birds of prey have increased.

Well-made stone butts blend well with the moorland landscape

Shooting on the moor in 1939

We have been immensely gratified by recent public recognition by important national organisations, such as the Nature Conservancy Council and the Royal Society for the Protection of Birds, of the value of the grouse-moor habitat to conservation generally. Look after the grouse and the moorland ecosystem should look after itself. Thus the considerable weight of the wildlife lobby is now firmly behind that of the economist in proclaiming the well-run grouse moor to be an essential element of upland Britain in the nineties.

Unfortunately, in devoting so much time to these very serious, though indisputably important issues, some Guns have almost forgotten how to enjoy their sport. They have become mere pawns in this ever-intense age of justification, when almost every activity is deemed to require explanation. Fortunately, we still have plenty of enthusiasts who regard simple enjoyment as the basic motivation. They rightly recognise that the economic and conservation spin-offs are fortuitous bonuses. We must not be too preoccupied with that small but dogged band of antis, most of whom profess to champion 'animal rights' but are really fired by age-old jealousy of privilege, especially more recently over the controversial issue of public access to moorland.

Additionally, there has been long-term conflict between grouse-shooters and farming and forestry in a land with a relatively small acreage per capita. Sheep- and tree-men have always demanded a fair share of the uplands, especially during periods

RAISED IN THE HIGHLANDS.

THE
FAMOUS GROUSE
FINEST SCOTCH WHISKY

QUALITY IN AN AGE OF CHANGE.

Ed Littlefield of the USA and loader await the action on The Duke of Roxburghe's Byrecleugh Estate

of strong government encouragement of national self-sufficiency. Fortunately, the recent slight decline in intensive farming, and the new interest in diversification of land use, promoted by the set-aside scheme, should do much to encourage the game and wildlife of both upland and lowland Britain.

Further encouragement comes from the increasing strength of the economy. Being largely a very social sport which inevitably attracts so-called 'high-achievers' to its ranks, game-shooting always grows most rapidly with the spread of affluence, so after ten years of continuous Conservative government it is hardly surprising that our sport has never been more popular. Driven shooting in particular offers the ideal vehicle for mixing business with pleasure. Grouse-shooting has always provided the cream of entertainment and there is no doubt that moorland relaxation has set the seal on many an important business deal.

SCOTT ADIE, LTD.

THE ROYAL SCOTCH WAREHOUSE

38, Conduit Street, London, W.1

WE
Specialise in
Sporting Garments
of every description.
Scotch Plaids,
Travelling Rugs
and Shawls.

❖ ❖

Best qualities at
Moderate Prices.

❖ ❖

Catalogue and
patterns
post free

❖ ❖

Telegrams :
Scott Adie, Piccy,
London.

Telephone :
Regent 3699.

The Strathvaich Cape

Has a great advantage over the ordinary shooting cape
with straps, having underneath a vest or sleeveless
jacket, thereby allowing the cape to be thrown back,
leaving the arms perfectly free and the chest quite
protected in cold and rainy weather. It is provided with
useful and roomy pockets.

Scott Adie advertisement (1924)

Illustrated
Catalogue
& Patterns
Post Free.

THE
BURBERRY
SUIT

adds materially to the enjoyment of shooting. Limb-
freedom, workmanlike design and protection, are great
aids in fine or foul weather.

For these reasons many shooting men meet at Burberrys
at dates in front of

"THE GLORIOUS TWELFTH"

Burberry Suits offer very stout resistance to wet and
cold without generating heat; retaining the perfect
ventilating qualities of unproofed fabrics.

BURBERRY SUITINGS

are choice and exclusive in character, texture and design
—delightful materials for the moors.

**The pleasures of shooting are made complete
by the ease, comfort and protection of the
well-fitting**

BURBERRY SHOOTING SUIT

Every Burberry garment bears the Burberry Trade Mark

BURBERRYS HAYMARKET
S.W.1 LONDON

8 & 10 BD. MALESHERBES PARIS ; & PROVINCIAL AGENTS

Burberrys Ltd.

Burberrys advertisement (1924)

Despite a general mood of optimism within the sport, we cannot afford complacency: even without a change of government all could change almost overnight. Of course we must continue to give our full support to the national shooting organisations *and* co-operate with conservationists whenever possible. But to gain even more supporters I believe we must place as much emphasis on the pure thrill of grouse-shooting as we already do on justifying its continuance. That is a prime objective of this book – to provide a taste of the unique atmosphere which will make people want to participate.

Given such a task as this, it is always both useful and stimulating to consider the subject through the eyes of our forebears, and to this end I begin with an extensive review of the history of grouse-shooting. Important technical innovations, such as with guns and ammunition, have been few and far between and for most people are far less interesting than human aspects of going to the moors, which comprise much of this review. Nonetheless, all relevant matters are discussed in detail.

One thing which certainly has changed remarkably since the advent of grouse-shooting is the study of natural history. Whereas amateur Victorians 'curious in nature' generally studied species in isolation, today we have a new breed of professional ecologists who must acknowledge the wider concept of habitat. In this respect the grouse is a most important species and I make no excuse for writing at length on its value to conservation generally as well as detailing its basic natural history.

I do not go into *great* detail on how to shoot grouse or even on which is the best gun: both subjects were adequately covered by precise Victorian authors and little has changed since then. Neither have I attempted to write reams on those aspects such as gundogs and basic keepering techniques. Only where changes have been significant do I venture into detail in these well-covered areas.

My aim has not been to focus on grouse moors and conservation in isolation, but as part of the very new and welcome 'green' philosophy which considers the purity of the natural environment and the quality of life to be at least as important as economic or political persuasions. In this I believe that we must always accommodate the hunter. Without the spirit of the chase human society will be immensely impoverished. The glorious grouse is still the King of Gamebirds and without its many loyal subjects the progressive kingdom of sporting conservation would soon return to the Dark Ages.

BRIAN P. MARTIN
Brook, Surrey
November 1989

1

From Obscurity to Poetry

The history of the grouse and grouse-shooting to 1800

With understandable pride, birdwatchers and sportsmen are always quick to point out that the red grouse is the only bird *species* confined to the British Isles. Sadly, this is not true as the bird is now recognised as a well-marked subspecies (race) (*Lagopus lagopus scoticus*) of the willow grouse (*Lagopus lagopus*), which is widespread in America and Eurasia. Neither is it the only *race* confined to these islands: others include the St Kilda wren (*Troglodytes troglodytes hirtensis*), Shetland wren (*T.t. zetlandicus*), Fair Isle wren (*T.t. fridariensis*), and the Outer Hebridean wren (*T.t. hebridensis*). Indeed, the Scottish crossbill (*Loxia curvirostra scotica*) has a greater claim to distinction in this field, in that some taxonomists still regard it as a full species (*L. scotica*) rather than a race of the parrot crossbill or common crossbill.

Whereas other races of willow grouse have white wings all year, our red grouse has little need to change to winter white in what is generally a relatively mild climate. But while the ancestors of today's 16–18 species of grouse are reasonably well represented in the fossil record, paleontologists cannot tell when the red grouse first acquired its distinctive plumage. Presumably a major factor was island isolation.

Today we can only guess at the grouse population of former times, but it seems likely that the bird was never so numerous as it has been since the introduction of driven shooting in the 1800s. Obviously, such a moorland species must have had a much more restricted range when most of the British Isles was still well wooded. And variations in climate would have caused both local and overall population fluctuations as they do to this day.

Primitive, nomadic man had little impact on grouse numbers, hunting only for the pot with inefficient weapons. But as he settled down to a sedentary existence he had to clear the forests about him to make way for his new crops and domesticated animals. In many areas this undoubtedly helped the spread of grouse from their former upland strongholds to newly created heather moors. Then the red grouse occurred in many areas of southern Britain from which it has long since disappeared.

Before the reign of Henry VIII, no English author mentioned grouse, whether red, black or white. The name grouse is probably derived from the French *greoche, greiche* and *griais*, meaning a spotted bird, the term *grows* being used to describe the red grouse in England in 1531. The common Scots name of moorfowl is recorded back to 1506. The term red game (*cf* black game) was recorded by John Ray in 1674 and the name red grouse was coined by Thomas Pennant in 1776 after the model of black grouse. This was adopted by most of Pennant's successors, and after Yarrell in 1843, became the unchallenged standard.

The folk name *gorcock* has been used for the male in northern England and Scotland since 1620 and is probably derived from an imitation of the barking call. But it was the Victorian writer Swainson who first interpreted the call as *Go, go, go, go back, go-o back*. Other regional names have included red ptarmigan, brown ptarmigan, heather cock, heath cock, moor poor or pout (Yorks for immature), moss-hen (Yorks for female), *coileach-fraoch* (Gaelic for heather cock), *cearc-fraoch* (Gaelic for heather hen), and muirfowl.

Rather surprisingly, the first English writer to allude to grouse, Dr William Turner (his 1544 book *Avium Praecipuarum Historia* was the first published book devoted entirely to birds), a native of Morpeth, expressed a doubt that the species be known in England, even though he was born near the Northumberland moors! Although his work was one of the first serious attempts to separate folklore and mythology from reality, and Turner tried hard to be accurate and introduce order into the naming of birds, he was obviously out of touch as far as grouse were concerned. In 1797, in his book *A History of British Birds*, Thomas Bewick of Newcastle stated that 'This bird is found in great plenty in the wild, heathy, and mountainous tracts in the northern counties of England; it is likewise common in Wales, and in the Highlands of Scotland.'

Before firearms were brought to a considerable degree of perfection, grouse would only be obtained by trapping or netting, chiefly at night. A bird-bolt, even when shot by a most skilled arbalister accompanied by a setting spaniel, was not likely to prove particularly destructive on a pack of grouse. Indeed, it is to be questioned if the most expert toxophilite could, with the bow and arrow, even allowing him dogs, bag a couple of brace during the season on the best preserved moors – unless he were to slay them sitting.

George Malcolm summed up the position in 1910: 'None of the earlier instruments and methods of the chase, with the exception perhaps of hawking or falconry, which are of high antiquity and go back to the Saxon occupation of Britain, could have been of avail for assault on our wary and nimble grouse.'

Scottish kings did not show the same interest in hunting as did the Norman kings of England, but there is ample evidence of the existence of several royal forests north of the border, and we have numerous detailed descriptions of royal or state visits to these. Indeed, the sixteenth century saw many Acts of the Scots Parliament for the seclusion and protection both of game and wild deer, the main focus of attention. In Scotland these early laws appear to have been administered with less selfishness and cruelty than in England. Nonetheless, the Scots statute book was disgraced by at least one such Act – 1551, cap 9: 'anent them that schuttis with gunnis at Deare and Wildfowle', which probably no Norman enactment surpassed in severity, for it actually inflicted the penalty of death, as well as confiscation of movables, upon the person who shot at these wild animals in the royal preserves. But by 1686, if not earlier, this Act had fallen into disuse.

The jealous protection afforded to the royal forests in Scotland is further exemplified by the Act of James VI, 1617, c 18, which proceeded upon the complaint 'that the Forests within the Realme are altogether wasted and decayed by Shielings, pastouring

Wild birds in a wild landscape. Painting by Archibald Thorburn (Courtesy of the Tryon Gallery)

of Horses, Mares, Cattel, Oxen, and other bestial'; and by a representation made by the Court of Session to the King 'against granting of new forests as prejudicial to the King's old forests and his lieges.'

At this time, just as today, the royal example was very important in giving the seal of approval to exclusive sport: but the nobility were untiring in their efforts to keep the best to themselves. For example, in 1528 King James V of Scotland

. . . made proclamation to all lords and barons, gentlemen, landwardmen, and freeholders, to compear at Edinburgh with a month's victual to pass with the King to danton (subdue) the thieves of Teviotdale, etc, and who warned all gentlemen that had good dogs to bring them, that he might hunt in the said country. The Earl of Argyle, the Earl of Huntley, the Earl of Atholl, and all the rest of the Highlands, did, and brought their hounds with them to hunt with the King. His Majesty therefore passed out of Edinburgh with 12,000 men, and hounded and hawked all the country and bounds.

Next summer, the King went to hunt in Atholl, accompanied by Queen Margaret and the Pope's ambassador, where he remained three days, 'most nobly entertained by the Earl'. There is also the case of Queen Mary of Scotland, who, with great state and circumstance, 'took the sport of hunting in the forest of Mar and Atholl in the year 1563'. Her great rival and relative, Elizabeth of England, also took the opportunity to engage in the same diversion: in 1595 she was present at a deer chase in Cowdray Park – no grouse there though.

Some people say these great royal hunts were largely to honour and humour local nobility, who went to great expense and trouble to impress the many important guests. Others maintain that they were really part of a rigorous, massive campaign against the people of those vast, secluded forests, whose depredations were occasionally troublesome. Yet there is no doubt that at least some of the early hunters were chiefly motivated by the spirit of the chase and the romance of lonely places.

In a Scots Act of Parliament, passed in 1621, in the reign of that enthusiastic though awkward sportsman, James VI, the '. . . buying and selling of wylde fowles, of the particular spaces [species] following are prohibited, under a penalty of a hundred pounds Scots.' The 'spaces' forbidden to be sold were: 'Pouttes, pairtrickes, muirfowles (red grouse), blacke-cocks, gray-hennes (female black grouse), termigantes, quailles, caperkaylles', etc. Previously, there had been little interest in sport with gamebirds, but the increasing sophistication and reliability of guns was changing all that.

The appearance of further game laws during the Restoration period emphasised the rise and dominance of the squirearchy, forcing yeomen and farmers to make unpopular sacrifices in order that the squire could shoot, just as the King, through forest laws, had supplanted all classes in preceding ages. Now shotgun shooting started to replace hawking as the gentleman's means of relaxation.

During Charles II's reign, it became more common, though not without much controversy, to shoot gamebirds in flight instead of simply stalking perched birds or walking them up with dogs. A Mr Wilson of Broomhead, Yorkshire, is said to have been the first person to shoot grouse on the wing, in about 1650, and Hunter's *Hallamshire, South Yorkshire* (Vol II, p183) refers to such shooting in 1687. Birds continued to be taken for food with lime, crossbow, traps, snares and nets, and nets were even used in sport. With the development of the shotgun it was gradually agreed that only certain species should be recognised as suitable for sport and classified as game. These included the red grouse and black cock. However, it is important to remember that before the eighteenth century only soldiers and a handful of diplomats had cause to venture into Scotland, and hardly anyone went there to sport. And without tourist income there was little incentive to improve roads or provide reasonable transport and accommodation.

Just as in other far-flung outposts of the Empire, it was chiefly military men who pioneered sport in wildest Britain of the eighteenth century. They had a natural affinity with guns and roughing it was second nature. And it did not take them long to discover the abundance of fish, fowl and furred game in the relatively untouched north, where virtually everything was cheap compared with London.

At that time there was still abundant wilderness, about a quarter of the country being heath and moor, and much of the remainder was medieval, with open fields of meadow and arable land adjoining gorse-covered common pasture. By 1760 less than a quarter million acres had been enclosed, the big transformation coming between 1750 and the General Enclosure Act of 1845, with most of the open fields disappearing in the sixty years of 'Farmer' King George III. Meanwhile, increasing demand for timber, started by medieval ship- and house-builders, accelerated the destruction of many woodlands, and moorlands were increasingly grazed by sheep, thus providing much more habitat suitable for grouse, especially in northern England.

But it was largely the romantic writings of poets and adventurers which suddenly generated increasing interest in northern sport. Among the first was Colonel Thomas Thornton (1757–1823), an English gentleman whose detailed accounts fired young bloods already aroused by romantics such as Ben Jonson, John Taylor and Walter Scott. His very popular book *A Sporting Tour Through the Northern Parts of England and Great Part of the Highlands of Scotland*, 1804, described several visits made in the 1780s. The amount of food supplies, powder and shot he shipped in or took by cart was prodigious. However, wealthy as he was, Thornton was still very much at the mercy of the weather in those muzzle-loading days. Of one windy outing he wrote:

Ordered dinner at three, intending to kill a few brace of cocks in the evening, when the moors would be dry and pleasant, which they were in two hours after the severest rain. Accordingly, after dinner, we went out, though the wind still blew very strongly, soon found plenty of game, but I shot very indifferently; and on my return, Mr Drighorn made the same complaint respecting himself. In the

Bewick wood engraving of the grouse (1797)

RED GROUSE.

rough grounds, where we shot in order to be more under the wind, our footing was very bad; and the birds which I intentionally rose upwind, when at the distance of thirty yards from the shooter, were always upon the wheel; besides which, not once in four times could the fire reach the powder, but was blown away; for the pans were so well contrived, that the powder was frequently not blown away when the fire was; these circumstances duly considered, I believe we were not so much in fault as we had suspected.

His money certainly ensured that he never went hungry – even when he thought he was roughing it he fared much better than most folk:

It was now past five and a dreadful rain. No encampment to be seen; eight Highland miles home; in the very heart of game; my powder, which I had been preparing, well dried; shot sufficient in my holsters for a days's sport; my dogs well fed on two cheeses and a large bowl of milk – Could there, to a sportsman, be any better measure adopted?

Matters thus adjusted, my landlady procured me a bowl of her best milk, to which I added a flask of very strong Jamaica rum; turned out of my canteen some ham and chicken, biscuits and Cheshire cheese, and, with fresh fuel, we became very merry.

In the interim, I despatched directly a herdsman to Raits, with orders to bring a bottle of rum, porter, and provisions, clean linen, etc.

A hodge podge, prepared at Raits, of moor-game, killed by the hawks, which, before the rain came on, had been fortunate; mutton and bacon were put on the fire in the kitchen bothie; I got dry things; Balacroon fished with the seine, and killed in ten minutes, at the tent door, a small salmon, and as many trout as would have fed double our number. At eight o'clock dinner was announced in the dining-room – it consisted of

A hodge podge

REMOVE

Boiled trout and salmon

Reindeer's tongue

Cold fowl

Brandered moor-game

SAUCES

Garlick, and capsicum vinegars

REMOVE

Cheshire cheese

Moor-game gizzards

Biscuits

LIQUORS

Port, Imperial, Jamaica rum punch, with fresh limes,

Porter, ale, etc.

We drank a little more than is usual, and slept very comfortably, ardently wishing for a fair day.

Among the most popular poets who wrote of the romance of moorland sport was Robert Burns (1759–96). In his 'Hunting Song' he paid tribute to red grouse ('moor-hen') cunning:

> The heather was blooming, the meadows were mawn,
> Our lads gaed a-hunting, ae day at the dawn,
> O'er moors and o'er mosses and mony a glen,
> At length they discovered a bonnie moor-hen.
>
> I rede (warn) you beware at the hunting, young men;
> I rede you beware at the hunting young men;
> Tak some on the wing, and some as they spring,
> But cannily steal on a bonnie moor-hen.
>
> They hunted the valley, they hunted the hill;
> The best of our lads wi' the best o' their skill;
> But still as the fairest she sat in their sight,
> Then, whirr! she was over, a mile at a flight.

But undoubtedly Sir Walter Scott (1771–1832) did more than any other writer to glorify grouseland and encourage the English to sport there. He, too, obviously enjoyed grouse-shooting and described it in the following poem:

> It's up Glenbarchan's braes I gaed,
> And o'er the bent of Killiebraid,
> And mony a weary cast I made,
>   To cuittle the moor-fowl's tail.
>
> If up a bonny blackcock should spring,
> To whistle him down wi' a slug in his wing,
> And strap him on to my lunzie string,
>   Right seldom would I fail.

By 'cuittle the moor-fowl's tail' he was alluding to gunshot peppering the rear of a red grouse as it sprang and made off in front. The 'lunzie string' would have been used to suspend his small bag of game from the waist.

Thus, as the eighteenth century drew to a close, the stage was set for the widespread development of grouse-shooting in northern Britain, which would move rapidly from being no more than the pastime of a few adventurers and eccentrics to the highly organised social sport of polite society, headed by the Royal Family.

2

A Proper Pursuit for Gentlemen

The development of grouse-shooting 1800–1850

When the nineteenth century dawned, hunting, shooting and fishing were still generally regarded as improper pursuits for the aristocracy, such rustic entertainment being left to the more adventurous minor gentry. Indeed, it was well into the 1800s before the owners of many estates even dreamed of taking to the field with a gun rather than send a keeper to secure game for the table. Certainly tramping the moor with a mightily long and heavy muzzle-loader, returning at nightfall to the most basic of accommodation, would not appeal to a man accustomed to every comfort. In any case, the grouse lived in such rough, inaccessible places, many of which could only be reached after interminable journeys by steamer, or bone-shaking carriages on the crudest of highways.

That great pioneering sportsman Colonel Hawker had no time for the faint-hearted. In his 1814 book *Instructions to Young Sportsmen* he wrote:

> Scotland is the best place for grouse shooting, as the heather there being much higher, they will lie closer than in Yorkshire and the other moors of England: add to which, the sport there, has, in many parts, the pleasant addition of blackcock and ptarmigan shooting. Such, however, is the misery of the Highland public houses, and particularly to our perfumed young men of fashion, that I have generally observed nine out of ten of them, however good may have been their sport, come home cursing and swearing most bitterly about their wooden berths, peat fires and oatmeal cakes.

At this time grouse were generally shot over dogs, small groups of friends tramping the moors with pointers and setters for relatively small bags, though shoots were certainly much more frequent than they are today. But the introduction of grouse driving, during the early years of the nineteenth century, was soon to revolutionise the sport, making it much more attractive to a wider cross-section of society.

There is a reference to driven grouse on the Bishop of Durham's Horsley Moor in 1803, but as some of the butts were in identical positions a century later they were probably the subject of careful study and may well have already been in use for at least several seasons. However, the first description of an informal type of driving relates to Mr Spencer Stanhope's moors on the Penistone Range in Yorkshire. One story is that when the owner became tired towards the end of the day, he used to sit in an old sandpit, and if his sons were walking nearby on Snailsden Moor he soon discovered that he got more shots in that position. Another tale is that the keeper there, George

Old sportsmen with pointers by Charles Henry Schwanfelger (1774–1837) (Courtesy of the Tryon Gallery)

Fisher, told the boys in the family to hide behind the rocks while he drove the low moor at Rayner Stones, Boadhill.

A few other people have also been credited with the invention of grouse driving, but it is most likely that the system merely evolved by chance in several parts of the country at about the same time. Others soon copied and tailored the method to suit local conditions, making it a regular practice from the mid-1830s.

There were certainly plenty of grouse in those days: Thornton had mentioned seeing a pack of 4,000 in 1782–3, though I suspect his enthusiasm encouraged exaggeration. More important are actual bag records: for example, in one week of September, 1817, the Earl of Fife's party bagged 821 brace and the Marquis of Huntly's team shot over 1,100 brace.

With more people interested in the sport there was inevitable increasing analysis of methods, some of which found its way into print. For example, in his 1821 book

The National Sports of Great Britain, Henry Alken described the need to deal with the old cock:

> Grouse lie best in fine weather, and may, in the early season, be followed from eight o'clock in the morning, as long as daylight lasts, provided the stamina and inclination of the gunner last also. A good refreshment at mid-day will forward this. Late in the autumn, from ten till two or three o'clock, is the longest shooting-day. Large shot, and the heaviest gun a man can conveniently carry, will then be found most effective, as the birds will run to a great distance. Sportsmen generally try to kill the old cock, which runs cackling away, in order to deceive and lead the pursuers from the brood. The cock being dead, the pack will lie until the dogs run upon them.

Grouse-shooting was obviously already important enough to warrant inclusion in Alken's book, but, especially in those early, undeveloped days, he was quick to point out that this was not a sport for cissies:

> The pursuit of moor-game is not to be classed with those gentle exercises which afford gratification, without fatigue to the sportsman; on the contrary it is one of the most laborious and fatiguing exertions which can be taken with the gun; and, indeed, is practised by those ardent votaries alone, who, in pursuit of their favourite diversions, are intimidated neither by long journeys perhaps in the first instance, nor by long walks or rides, beneath a burning sun, over moor, mountain, and bog, and in the roughest ways which matted heath, loose stones, concealed cavities in the earth, and obstructions of all kinds can produce.

Despite the hardships, however, the Twelfth was already deemed glorious by many devotees. (The 12 August–10 December season was set by Act of Parliament in 1773, though for many years flagrantly disregarded in remote regions.) The excitement and anticipation of the night before (the so-called 'Eve of St Grouse') was described in *The Oakleigh Shooting Code* of 1833:

> When the Guns are expected to be numerous, it is decided to be on the ground as soon as it is light enough to commence operations in a fair way. Birds may be killed above the horizon long before sun-rise; but the sportsman's rule is never to fire, until the morning is so far advanced that he can plainly distinguish them in their flight against the dark hill-side. They arrange to breakfast at three, (calculating the time by their watches, and not by the house-clock, which may have a way of going peculiar to itself) and to be on the ground before four; as the greatest number of birds are killed between four and six, and when there are many contesting for the prize it is folly to throw away a chance. If the moor is strictly preserved, and no Guns are expected but their own, they determine not to disturb the birds until six, since birds lie better during the day, when not disturbed early in the morning. The question being disposed of, enquiry is made

whether the dogs have been fed, and the shooters who intend killing their full complement of birds retire before eleven, (a late hour, bye the bye, in the vicinity of a moor), lest they should not feel as they could wish in the morning; and this is the more necessary if they be not members of a Temperance Society. Every bed is speedily occupied, and the retainers lie on sofas, elbow-chairs, or whatever else presents itself; but the God of slumber is invoked in vain. The soldier before battle is not more anxious as to the result of the morrow, than is the sportsman on the night of the 11th of August.

In later years a 9 or even 10 o'clock start would become the custom, except for those few Victorian big Shots who deliberately went out for record bags and needed all the daylight going. Indeed, the early start was frowned upon as early as 1840, by John Colquhoun in *The Moor and the Loch*:

Most young Shots are not content unless they are on the moor by peep of day on the long-anticipated 12th of August. And what is the result? They have found and disturbed most of the packs before they have well fed, and one half will rise out of distance, and fly away unbroken. Had the moor been left quiet till eight or nine o'clock, fair double shots might have been obtained at almost every pack, and many would have been scattered for the evening shooting. It will generally be found that if two equal Shots, upon equal moors, uncouple their dogs, one at five o'clock, and the other at eight, and compare notes at two in the afternoon, the lazy man will have the heaviest gamebag, and his ground will be in the best order for the deadly time of the day, to say nothing of his competitor's disadvantage from having fruitlessly wasted his own strength and that of his dogs, when many of the packs would not allow him to come within reach. My advice, therefore, to the young grouse-shooter, is always to wait till the dew is dry on the heather. If he starts at eight o'clock, and travels the moor as he ought, there is time enough before dark to put his powers to the proof, however he may pique himself upon them.

There is no record of the letting of grouse-shooting before the first quarter of the nineteenth century was well advanced, and up to the middle of the century the rents obtained for even exclusive shooting rights were quite insignificant. Highland lairds first opened their eyes to the possibilities when cattle had to give way to sheep. They found that with sensible management it was possible to crop both grouse and sheep on one moor, and the income from sheep in lean grouse years was always welcome. In 1837 only eight grouse-moors were let in Scotland, but by the end of the century this had grown to thousands.

As the century wore on, sport on the moors was increasingly sought after by the landed gentry and others possessing wealth and leisure enough to indulge. The romantic poesy and tales of Sir Walter Scott and glowing descriptions by other writers, of the stirring scenic beauty and grandeur of the Highlands, awakened widespread desire to visit and explore the mysterious hinterland. But in the 1830s, before the modern means of locomotion, just £20 was paid for a year's shooting over 50,000 acres. It needed the advent of the railways, to allow shooters to reach the moors regularly and in comparative safety, to stimulate competition. But even then the amounts paid for the small number of moors let were insignificant compared with those paid by sheep farmers, then at the peak of their prosperity. During the early nineteenth century rising prices made farming an attractive proposition, and as more land in England went under the plough, those many new followers of shooting had to look north for truly wild sport. By the 1830s, grouse-shooting was quite fashionable and many Englishmen regularly visited northern moors as a refuge from London life. Autumn relaxation in the country rapidly became an established part of the social scene.

Unfortunately, as economics played an increasingly important part in grouse-shooting, there was undue emphasis on bags, consistent records helping to maximise income. But even in the first half of the nineteenth century there were those alert to the dangers of commercialisation. For example, in his 1849 book *A Tour in Sutherland*, Charles St John wrote:

> Although, like others, I am excessively fond of this sport, yet I care little for numbers slain; and when following it independently and alone, am not occupied solely by the anxiety of bagging so many brace. My usual plan when I set out is to fix on some burn, some cool, grassy spring, or some hill summit which commands a fine view, as the extremity of my day's excursion. To this point then I walk, killing what birds come in my way, and after resting myself and dogs, I return by some other route. Undoubtedly the way to kill the greatest number of grouse is to hunt one certain tract of ground closely and determinedly; searching every spot as if you were looking for a lost needle, and not leaving a yard of heather untried. This is the most killing system, as every practised grouse-shooter knows; but to me it is far less attractive than a good stretch across a range of valley and mountain, though attended with fewer shots. I am also far more pleased by seeing a brace of good dogs do their work well, and exhibiting all their fine instinct and skill, than in toiling after twice the number when hunted by a keeper, whose only plan of breaking the poor animals in is to thrash them until they are actually afraid to use half the wonderful intellect which nature has given them.

Another unfortunate aspect of increasing economic pressure on sport was the ascendancy of poaching. A public eager to consume game in large quantities, however obtained, made a mockery of the seasons. In his 1843 book *A History of British Birds*, William Yarrell remarked:

> The quantity of red grouse supplied to the London market only, could the number be ascertained, must be enormous, when it is considered that from the second week in August up to the end of the first week in March, of every year, the supply is large and constant. The females now to be seen in the shops of the

High grouse population densities depend on the underlying rock as well as heather maintenance. Painting by Archibald Thorburn (Courtesy of the Tryon Gallery)

London poulterers [7 March, 1840], have begun to assume the plumage peculiar to the breeding season. These have been killed very recently, and I have observed within the last three years, that a considerable portion of the birds I have examined bore no marks of having been shot, and have probably been caught by sliding loops of horse hair set up across their paths in the heather.

But other, less knowledgeable writers have done a great disservice in perpetuating the romantic image of poachers. These included Charles St John in his *Wild Sports and Natural History of the Highlands* (1846):

When a party of them sleep out on the hillside, the manner of arranging their couch is as follows: if snow is on the ground, they first scrape it off a small space; they then all collect a quantity of the driest heather they can find. The next step is for all the party excepting one to lie down close to each other, with room between one couple for the remaining man to get into the ranks when his duty is done; which is to lay all the plaids on the top of his companions, and on the plaids a quantity of long heather; when he has sufficiently thatched them in, he creeps into the vacant place, and they are made up for the night. The coldest frost has no effect on them, when bivouacking in this manner. Their guns are laid dry between them, and their dogs share their masters' couch.

Yet no trifling matter such as poaching would hold back the sport's progress now. As the first half of the nineteenth century drew to a close, vastly improved communications by road and rail, coupled with increasing difficulty in securing sport further south, made grouse moors highly desirable properties. In addition, the relatively unspoilt northern hills generally offered a wider variety of quarry birds, as well as plenty of deerstalking, and fishing for salmon and trout in unpolluted waters. In 1848 Queen Victoria leased Balmoral from Lord Mar (she purchased the estate in 1852), and when Prince Albert took to shooting grouse and deer with such enthusiasm the sport was firmly established as a proper pursuit for gentlemen of every rank.

The glorious grouse had made its mark: it was recognised as a truly wild quarry without sporting equal in Britain, and its home was a place for bodily and spiritual refreshment, well away from the grime and commerce of the industry which consumed a nation seeking world dominance. Craven described the mood of the period in his 1846 book *Recreations in Shooting*:

There is no species of rural sport of which the characteristics are so picturesque and so wild as those of grouse-shooting. Fox-hunting and woodcock-shooting both lead their disciples remote from cities, but though they be wild sports, the season of the year peculiar to them divests the scenes in which they are pursued of all the attributes of picturesque or beautiful. It is the golden time of the year to the young amateur of the trigger.

For Craven, 'Caledonia, stern and wild' was

. . . the chosen land of the grouse-shooter. Few attempt the sport in the Welch mountains, except such as happen to be to the matter born – the native "Taffies" – or their guests in "the season of the year". In Scotland, shooting-quarters are as commonly let to yearly tenants or on lease, as the use of the land is hired out to the farmer.

But such preoccupation with Scotland owed as much to the imagery of Walter Scott as it did to sporting potential because before too long many moors south of the Border would rank among the country's finest.

3

The Search for Value

*With breechloaders came bigger bags, bigger rents and increasing pressure
on poachers and predators in the 1850–70 period*

The introduction of the breechloading shotgun in the 1850s was to transform grouse-shooting. It gave the rapidity of firing which made driven shooting really worthwhile, encouraging the use of double guns with a loader and stimulating the development of much larger bags. Rather surprisingly, the introduction of driven shooting brought about a sharp increase in grouse bags out of all proportion to that expected through increased firepower. Probably the main reason for this is that old birds tend to come over the Guns first and a larger proportion of them are killed than would be the case if the birds were walked-up. This is good for the stock because the older birds are more territorial and combative and interfere considerably with the nesting of younger birds. By driving, the danger of killing off whole broods is obviated, especially during the early part of the season, when walking-up can easily wipe out an entire covey as the birds rise in twos or threes. Driving also moves the birds around more and refreshes the blood of local stock, and there is no doubt that through thinning the breeding stock, driving has reduced the incidence of disease.

The new breechloaders were also much shorter and lighter than previous guns, making them more attractive to a wide range of genteel folk. Self-contained cartridges were more reliable and easier to cope with than the old powder- and shot-flasks of the muzzle-loaders, and there was no longer any need for 'tiresome traipsing about the wet, cold moors where grouse spend most of their time hiding.'

Yarrell marvelled

> . . . that a species which furnishes sport to so many, and to such an extent, besides those taken cladestinely, should continue to exist in such quantities in the country. The Earl of Strathmore's gamekeeper was matched for a considerable sum to shoot 40 brace of moorgame in the course of the 12th of August, upon his lordship's moors in Yorkshire; he performed it with great ease, shooting 43 brace by 2 o'clock.

And back in 1801 'a gentleman in Inverness-shire shot 52 brace in one day, never killing a bird sitting, or more than one bird at one shot.'

A birdwatcher first, Yarrell probably failed to recognise the increasingly important role of the gamekeeper in managing the habitat for the benefit of grouse so that much larger bags could be taken without depleting the breeding stock. However, he did note the relationship between bag size and the date:

At the first of the season the young birds lie close, particularly where the heath is high and strong, affording excellent sport after a favourable breeding season, and the newspapers frequently record the great numbers that are favourably located; but as the season advances, the birds get strong, and from being disturbed, become wild, and the families uniting to form packs, are then very difficult to get shots at.

But he did not suggest, as other, misinformed commentators had done, that driving had been introduced primarily to get within range of birds that had become too wild to walk-up!

A better-informed sporting naturalist of the mid-nineteenth century was A. E. Knox, who gave an interesting account of the grouse in his 1850 book *Game Birds and Wild Fowl*:

The great stronghold of the species is of course the Highlands of Scotland, where its preservation is carried to such an extent, and the rights of shooting let at such high rents, that in spite of the annual slaughter during the first three weeks of the season – far surpassing in this respect even the battue of the southron – there appears to be no immediate prospect of its extermination or even material reduction, although, speaking as a naturalist rather than a sportsman, it cannot but be a matter of regret that the excessive protection of the grouse involves the indiscriminate slaughter of so many interesting birds and quadrupeds now becoming exceedingly rare among us.

As an example of over-zealous keepering, Knox quoted a list of 'vermin' destroyed on the celebrated Highland property of Glengary, between Whitsunday 1837 and Whitsunday 1840, previous to the purchase of the estate by Lord Ward:

The slaughter was carried into effect by numerous keepers, who received not only liberal wages but extra rewards, varying from £3 to £5, according to their success in the work of extermination of: foxes, wild-cats, martin-cats, pole-cats, stoats, weasels, badgers, otters, house-cats going wild, white-tailed sea eagles, golden eagles, ospreys or fishing eagles, blue hawks or peregrine falcons, kites – commonly called salmon-tailed gledes, marsh harriers or yellow-legged hawks, goshawks, orange-legged falcons, hobby hawks, common buzzards, rough-legged buzzards, honey buzzards, kestrels or red-hawks, merlin hawks, ash-coloured or long blue-tailed hawks, hen harriers or ring-tailed hawks, jer-falcons or toe-feathered hawks, carrion and hooded crows, ravens, horned owls, common fern owls [probably short-eared owls rather than nightjars], golden owls [probably white or barn owls], magpies.

Knox was equally concerned about the depredations of poachers:

After the month of August grouse are better able to take care of themselves,

'Amongst the Heather' by Archibald Thorburn, one of Britain's most celebrated gamebird painters

Grouse eggs are subject to considerable colour variation

Rather stylised Victorian painting of the red grouse from Rev F. O. Morris's book A History of British Birds

and, although comparatively safe from the legalized shooter during the winter, great quantities then fall victims to the Highland poacher, especially when snow is on the ground, as they pack together in considerable numbers, and expose themselves on any turf-stack, wall or bank that happens to rise above the surface of the moor. They are also snared, and occasionally netted; although, from a habit in these birds of scattering at the approach of the fowler, this last mode of capture is less profitable than might be imagined, and it is certain that various strategems are then in vogue – when, by the way, the keepers and watchers are generally dismissed, instead of being doubled as they ought to be – for the London market is regularly supplied, up to the middle of March, with birds which exhibit no signs of having perished from a gunshot wound . . .

Like so many Victorian naturalists, Knox was also very aware of problems within the sport other than those directly affecting other wildlife:

Thanks to railways and the rapidity of steam communication between London and Inverness, the acquisition of a first-rate moor is now only a question of money; and the opulent citizen who but yesterday was buried in the pages of his ledger, amid the smoke of Threadneedle Street, may find himself tomorrow regularly located in his Highland lodge, bracing his relaxed nerves with the mountain breeze, or despatching baskets of grouse for the hospitable tables of his less fortunate friends in the city. It may be observed, however, that bitter disappointment not infrequently follows in the track even of the wealthy Saxon. The right of sporting may comprise several thousand acres, yet not contain as many score of grouse, which perhaps have been shot down to the very verge of extinction by the former tenant, who has probably availed himself of his right to reap the reward of a long period of care and protection during the last season of his occupation. Such a result, however, may generally be avoided by a previous inquiry on the spot, while to obtain a 'well-stocked moor' in the modern acceptation of the term, it is advisable to secure the tenancy for several successive seasons.

In Ireland, 'the system of letting the manors' had not yet been introduced. But Knox preferred the sport there for its 'admixture of woodcocks, snipe, plover, and wild-ducks . . . the character of a day's shooting depending rather upon the variety of the spoil than upon the numbers of the slain.'

He remembered with great affection when in the early years of the nineteenth century he went to a wild tract of north-west Ireland for his first acquaintance with the 'hen of the heath', then also known as 'Cark na fre' in the remote parts of Connaught. The moor had 'a fair head of grouse' through 'the management of an intelligent Scotch keeper who employed watchers.' When the road 'terminated', all communication with the lodge was

. . . carried on by means of natives from the nearest village, whose limbs, unshackled by shoe or stocking, displayed an enviable activity in traversing the rough, broken grounds; and whose light-hearted merriment and good temper contributed not a little to the pleasures of the expedition. A few of these only were selected as markers and ordered to be in their respective positions among the hills before day-break on the following morning; while the rest were despatched the same evening with sundry articles of heavy baggage to the lodge, and instructed to meet us on the morrow, with a relay of dogs, near the borders of a little lough, which we expected to reach early in the afternoon.

So the party walked-up with setters and bagged 'a sufficient sprinkling to satisfy our most sanguine expectations', including 'cock, grouse, golden plover, snipe and, with the assistance of a water-spaniel, several ducks and teal.' In other words, it was a good, old-fashioned moorland walk-up of the type coming back into fashion today.

Another respected ornithologist who expressed concern over habitat loss as early as the mid-nineteenth century was the Reverend F. O. Morris. In his book *A History of British Birds* (1851–7) he wrote of the grouse:

The red bird, like the Red Indian, gives way before the inroads of cultivation, and flourishes only where nature is yet to be seen in her primitive aspect. Attempts have been made to re-establish the ancient Briton in Devon, Dorset, Sussex and Surrey, but in vain; aboriginal inhabitants, like my own ancestors in ages long gone by, before Roman, Saxon, Dane or Norman had set foot on the soil, when once driven into the fastnesses of Wales and the wild districts of the country, there alone can they maintain their tribe.

Engraving of grouse driving in Derbyshire (1880s)

However, as far as the average sportsman was concerned, there were grouse enough for everybody, and now that the bird was classified as game the nation would ensure that parliamentary business finished in time for the Glorious Twelfth. Everyone who was anyone wanted to be well informed as to the best moors and every year the ever-growing band of sportsmen eagerly awaited news of the season's prospects as well as the first shoot reports.

To begin with, general newspapers were the chief source of fieldsport reports, but in 1853 the specialist gap in the market was filled with the launch of *The Field*, grandly subtitled *The Country Gentleman's Newspaper*. For this new publication, the brainchild of Jorrocks' creator R. S. Surtees and owned by the proprietors of *Punch*, grouse-shooting was an ideal interest and there is no doubt that the journal was to play an important part in the sport's development.

At first, *The Field*, too, concentrated on gathering grouse reports from local newspapers such as the *Carlisle Patriot* and the *Montrose Standard*. In their 26 August, 1854 issue, they stated that grouse were selling for 5s a brace at Penrith, but up to 6s in Carlisle. 'Large quantities have found their way to the dealers,' but 'there is no doubt that the lion's share still falls to the poachers.'

Bags were small in the first week of that season. For example:

On Rodrip-fell, near Alston-moor, on the 12th, despite the rain, Mr Jos Richardson, of Penrith, wine-merchant, killed 10½ brace. On Melmerby-moor, Mr S. Carmalt, of Penrith, on the 12th, only killed 3 brace, but on Monday he was more fortunate and bagged 10 brace.

But at Lochlee Lord Panmure killed 64 brace, his nephew 43 and Col Ferguson 18. The Duke of Buckingham, Mr Laverock and friends had 'first-rate bagging, in a few hours upwards of 100 brace'. From Strathdon we learn that the hills and corries 'at an early hour resounded with a rattling fire' on the 12th. 'At Newe, McHardy, Sir Charles's head gamekeeper, went out at a late hour and shot 13 brace.'

From Perthshire came news that:

A very great number of sportsmen have passed through Perth en route for the north; in fact, many more, we believe, than for several years past; and we learn that the Perthshire moors are all let, except those in the possession of their proprietors. Since the commencement of the shooting the coaches and other conveyances from the Highlands have not brought nearly the usual number of game-boxes to town, as compared with former years. On the Monday, the London mail-train carried about 50 boxes of grouse to the south. The Duke of Wellington coach, from Inverness, brought 50 boxes to Perth in the evening; and on Tuesday 68 boxes. On Tuesday morning the Duke of Wellington van arrived here with 61 boxes and on Wednesday with 78.

At Logiealmond the Earl of Mansfield killed 83 brace of birds with his own gun . . . at Dalnaspidal, on Saturday, Mr Stirling Crawford and party killed 150 brace, but on the 14th they had 320 brace.

On 2 September, *The Field* reported:

> The moors continue to yield abundant sport, and the birds never were in finer
> condition at this season of the year. Mr Ackroyd and Mr Edwards have had very
> regular and satisfactory sport at Glenshere, Mr A. having killed 280 brace and
> Mr E. 230 brace. On no day did they fire a shot before noon. The Duke of
> Richmond's party, at Glenfiddich, shot 1200 brace in 7 days.

However, 'the success offered to sportsmen on the moors has checked their ardour
in making for the forests and very few deer or stags have yet been shot.' At Carlisle
grouse were down to 4s a brace.

In the following week it was reported that 'Mr Finnie and his party, at Glentruin,
have shot 1,040 brace up to August 26, being an average of 25 brace per bag every
day.' Other game shot included hares, blackgame, plovers, roebuck, snipe and the
occasional pheasant. By 23 September 'The notes from the moors are becoming more
scanty. The fact is, the birds are so very strong that he is a fortunate sportsman indeed
who can manage to make a fair day's bag in double the usual time, The sport is,
accordingly, very harassing.'

As the sport grew, fostered by increasing wealth and publicity, so, too, did *The
Field*'s coverage. By 1858, not only was there sufficient interest to warrant extensive
notes well before the season, but also to justify close examination of diverse subjects
from grouse disease to grouse transportation.

The 17 July, 1858 issue attributed the great scarcity of birds that year not only to
disease but also to the fact that moors were over-exploited and let at high rents

> . . . with flourishing accounts as to the stock . . . at a time when they were
> worn out and exhausted and ought rather to have been nursed and protected
> than subjected to the incursion of the keen sportsman, who, dissatisfied because
> he had paid a high rent for prospects of sport which had not been realised, killed
> every bird he could find.

So *The Field* advocated an improved system of letting: 'If any reasonable amount of
seed be left on the ground, two years' forebearance, with proper care and protection,
will bring round most moors and other shooting grounds, provided the breeding
seasons prove favourable.'

That week, *The Field* also reported that grouse were still being sold in advance of
the season. In and around Alston they were available at 5s a brace and they had even
been sending them to London since 1 July!

The important subject of 'packing and transmitting grouse surplus to requirements'
was a major topic for *The Field*'s 24 July, 1858 issue. Boxes sent by rail were paid for
according to weight so planks had to be 'thoroughly seasoned and not too thick'. The
suggested system of manufacture was as follows:

> An application should be made on the part of the keeper at the nearest saw mills
> for planks of the following dimensions, and if about £2 be expended there will

be sufficient material to make from 150 to 200 boxes of various dimensions: some of one-fourth of an inch in thickness, and 13 inches broad, for tops or covers; some of three-eighths of an inch thick and 13 broad, for bottoms; the others of ½ inch thick and 6 broad, for sides; these latter being the recipients of all the nails must of necessity be thicker than the other two. If boxes are required exclusively for grouse, 4in will be sufficiently wide for the side planks. With materials thus secured, a good carpenter can make from 12 to 15 boxes per day and the entire cost will not far exceed 6d per box.

Boxes should always be ready when required and never 'on the exigency of the moment'. Use of green wood of unnecessary thickness would mean that carriage to London of a five-brace box would probably cost 10 or 12s instead of 3s 6d. And

> . . . if you wish your birds to reach their destination in good condition they must not be pressed together. Hops are sometimes used in packing, and are excellent as preservative; but charcoal powdered, and mixed with a little pepper, will answer the purpose equally as well, and is a cheaper material. This should be introduced under the wings and into the mouths of birds; and if quite cold at the time of packing, will remain good for several days. Fresh-killed birds packed before they are quite cold will not keep 24 hours.

There was also a dearer, compartmented box which took up to twenty brace – one brace in each compartment – and with which 'neither heather nor paper are required'. Each brace was 'placed with their feet towards each other, their heads lying in an outward direction'. The advantage of such separation was that 'if one bad bird be accidentally introduced he will not spoil the others'. But even with these the charcoal/pepper mix was recommended, 'and before putting the lids on a small quantity of heather just sufficient to keep the birds in their place'. Finally,

> . . . it is always advisable to nail two addresses on each box, one on the side and one on the top, as the latter is occasionally torn off or damaged either on board the steamer or in the luggage-van of the train by heavier boxes . . . The date and 'Perishable' should be legibly written, in which case railway companies are responsible in the event of the game being spoilt in consequence of the delay.

Some of the new breechloaders and ammunition were having teething troubles, and understandably also met with sales resistance among traditionalists. *The Field* for 21 August, 1858 reported on the day on the Ayrshire moors when D. Gray watched his friend Hunter shoot with a breechloader by Mortimer of Edinburgh:

> A better killer I seldom ever saw; but he had frequent mistakes, arising from the lead escaping out of the barrel from the discharge of the first barrel, and missed many double shots in consequence. He had also two miss-fires from the cap slipping out of the case.

In the same issue it was reported that Lord Stamford, with two friends, opened the season on the Staley moors, Cheshire, '. . . in excessive heat, rendering the pursuit after the feathered tribe a work of labour; but the soul-stirring call of the grouse, as it echoed along the valley, urged the sportsman through the heather in spite of all obstacles.' But they had 'extraordinary sport', Lord Stamford killing 44 on the 12th (a thunderstorm caused the party to stop on 96 at the end of the morning), 168 on the 13th and 150 on the 14th. The party's three-day total was 349 brace. Game on the 3,000-acre moors was 'strictly preserved, and, except these few days shooting they are kept perfectly quiet; no sheep or other animals allowed to graze upon them.'

Increasingly, the subject of rents and getting value for money was being raised by readers. In the 4 September, 1858 issue R. Pigot reported that he had paid about £100 a year for 7,300 acres at Lumphanan, Aberdeenshire, producing some 800 head of game of all types, but 'the country is infested with turnpike gates – 8d for a horse and gig every six miles, 1s 6d for a 2-horse carriage.' And 'in a year's time a railroad will run along the edge of the lake, in a great measure destroying the shootings altogether.'

Other rents at that time included £180 for 20,000 acres at Scardroy, near Beauly, Ross-shire, and £500 for 55,000 acres at Achary Moors, Lairg, Sutherland.

'Detonator' of Perth wrote:

Proprietors and tenants of moors are now, I assume, pretty well satisfied that nothing but careful preserving can keep up rents and sport when in moderation. To obtain the object all have in view, preserving must not be confined to keeping off poachers during the shooting season and killing vermin, though both are most important. The greatest destruction takes place out of season, when the birds are comparatively easily snared or shot; and the disgraceful readiness with which the illegal sale of game is made safe by the public, who are the purchasers, affords the great encouragement to that class of the community who are too lazy to work, and too dishonest to refrain from taking what is not strictly watched. It is the receivers of stolen and contraband goods that are the promoters of crime. If the rich did not buy game illegally obtained, there would be no poaching, and no destruction of it out of season; but when we know that not only at aldermen's feasts, but at the tables of noblemen – even at the white-bait dinners of the Cabinet – grouse, under the *sobriquet* of Scotch pigeons, are served, and eaten with the greater gusto, that they have been stolen, it is not surprising that the trade has increased to an extent, including even the sale of grouse eggs, as to threaten the annihilation of the breed and sport altogether.

To combat this, 'Detonator' advocated prosecution by all at every opportunity, suggesting that all sportsmen and proprietors join in

. . . one great association to trace out and prosecute to the uttermost any person . . . Efforts should be especially directed to stop grouse carriage, receipt and sale after the season closes. The carriers, game dealers, coach-guards, steamers, railways, hotels, are the great promoters of the illicit traffic . . .

Engraving of stalking grouse on the stooks (1880s)

The penalty for having grouse in possession after the permitted time was then £5, but

> . . . the words of the Act allow no discretionary power with reference to the time or place, where or when, the game may have been obtained. The prosecutor, or party giving the information, is entitled to half the penalty, which would go far to pay the expenses, as the parties prosecuted would generally be able to pay such a fine.

In Ireland, an equally serious problem, which has remained to this day, was that of insufficient keepers. On 18 September, 1858 William Young wrote to *The Field* from Connemara:

> In this district there is a great extent of ground well fitted for grouse, but from the total want of preservation (there not being a single qualified keeper in the district) the birds are so scattered and so few in number that to make a decent bag is a simple impossibility. There is a remarkable difference between the grouse of this country and those of the North of Ireland and Scotland, both of which countries I have shot in – namely, the Connemara grouse are perfectly tame the

whole season through, usually letting gun and dogs within 10 yards before rising; whereas those of the latter countries, from this week till the end of the season, can hardly be approached with dogs.

Another Irish correspondent, Colonel J. Whyte, wrote on 16 October, warning against being 'too liberal to Paddy in order to secure his gratitude and co-operation'. Whyte had let some of the principal farmers have coursing rights on his land, assuming that their interest would help his game preservation. But lack of birds and scattered coveys later aroused his suspicion and the discreet expenditure of a little cash moistened with whiskey soon laid bare the rotten spot.

It appeared that the amiable gentleman to whom I had accorded the right of coursing used to allow the scamps of the county to take their dogs out in the breeding season (church time being generally chosen), and amuse themselves by starting the little cheepers with their colly dogs – the greyhounds being trained to snap them up as soon as they fluttered above the heather.

Ireland is in truth a most difficult country to preserve game in, not because the people are poachers, for, except in cases like this, the frieze-coated man is rarely a poacher by trade (it is a class above them that takes that line), but because of the numerous small farms into which the lands are divided, and because every Irishman on each of these holdings thinks it necessary, in addition to his wife and ten children, to keep one, two or more curs of the most useless and offensive description. It is not only the mischief that these brutes do by destroying game themselves (and as young Paddy never dreams of going out to dig a potato or drive home the cow without the cur at his heels, smelling and prying into every bush – the amount is by no means small – in fact, more extensive, in my opinion, than that committed by every other description of vermin put together); but beyond this, they are the cause of a still greater evil, it being impracticable to destroy the hooded crow or weasel without coming across these beastly curs; and that infallibility produces an ill feeling in the breast of the owner – the thing of all others that for a thousand reasons, one is most anxious to avoid.

Of all the pests that Ireland contains, and we have to the full as many as our neighbours, there is none to equal cur dogs. You cannot drive or ride 100 yards without one of these brutes snapping at your horse's heels. They roam in bands at night like jackals, snarling and fighting round your doors, destroying your pets, your lambs, your game . . . Why is it that Chancellors of the Exchequer will not fill their balance sheet, and confer a blessing on that country at the same time, by a tax of 10s on each dog, instead of sending us back to the old days of still-hunting and potheen-making, as has been done by raising the duty on whiskey?

Not everyone sympathised with Whyte, however. In the following issue of *The Field* 'Hold Fast' wrote:

An English or Scotch landlord would perhaps say 'Shoot down every cur on the estate'; but if he lived in a country where threatening notices were common, and murder a trade, he would probably subside like others into a state of quiescence, or leave a country in disgust in which the laws were so badly administered. Offend or quarrel with a man in Ireland and it is 'war to the knife'; if shooting at a man from behind a hedge or turf-stack to satiate a vindictive spirit deserves so honest a term. If Col Whyte will extirpate the Ribandmen, Ireland will go ahead, and many obstacles will disappear that keep the sister country behind in a social as well as in a sporting point of view.

Also that week, the question of Ireland's different grouse-shooting season was under discussion. Representative of many letters received at *The Field* office was that from 'A Good Observer':

Sir – I sincerely hope that you may not be induced by any of my countrymen to advocate a change in our grouse day from 20th to 12th August. Were the season to commence 8 days earlier, what slaughter would be committed even during that short period! and grouse would consequently soon become extinct in Ireland; for it so happens in our changeable climate, we seldom have two such fine summers in succession as the past.

Meanwhile, in Scotland the subject of rates was causing disquiet. By 14 October, in Caithness, Col Whitelocke and Charles Turner, on the Clyth Moors, Latherton, near Lybster, had killed 980 head of grouse, 40 blackgame, 48 partridges, 12 snipe, 1 plover, 'hares of both kinds 35', and 4 rabbits – total 1,121 head. They paid a rental of £100 for some 10,000 acres. Whitelocke wrote:

All the grouse were fine birds; I killed no cheepers . . . I quit these moors in consequence of my landlord raising the rent 25 per cent, in addition to which I am assessed 1s 10d in the pound for poor rates. Good as the sport is here, being in such an out of the way part of the world, I think I paid quite enough for it.

Five years later the arguments over fair rentals continued, but now better-educated sportsmen were sensibly discussing the matter in relation to heather-burning and cyclical grouse disease. On 22 August, 1863, *The Field* published an important letter from that distinguished sportsman Horatio Ross, who, among many other achievements, is credited with killing 82 grouse with 82 cartridges on his 82nd birthday – with a muzzle-loader!:

While rents were rising grouse were steadily diminishing in numbers owing to grouse disease and unrestricted heather-burning. I have no sympathy with the gentlemen from the Stock Exchange, and from the large manufacturing towns, who pay extravagant rents . . . and who have so materially caused the present high rents; they are not sportsmen; they look on a trip to the Highlands as a sort of monster picnic, and whether they shoot diseased birds or healthy birds is a matter of very little consequence.

But Ross sympathised with

. . . good sportsmen to whom the expenditure of £500 or £600 a year is a matter of consequence. At the moment a moor of any extent cannot be rented for less than £300 or £400 a year. The taxes, keepers, travelling to the moor, etc cannot be put down as less than £200 a year – in all £500 or £600 a year.

He pointed out that on an average seven-year lease there would be no sport in three years, so he would actually pay £875–975 each season.

Ross considered *controlled* burning to be essential in fighting grouse disease and pointed to the example of Lord Dalhousie's Forfarshire moor of 300,000 acres:

He does not permit any of his tenants to burn heather; he employs his own servants to do so, and they annually burn it in long strips. Two years ago disease appeared after septennial periods on his moors but did little damage . . . Burning should not be left in the hands of the sheep farmer.

In conclusion, Ross said that Highland proprietors were no worse than southerners, but 'they had been rather spoiled by the great demand for both sheep grazings and shootings.' Shooters had recklessly bid against each other 'without making inquiries as to grouse disease.' He advocated a new renting system to take account of the three 'dead' years in the seven-year cycle.

In the following week, *The Field* pointed to the relatively good value to be had in Wales. There were plenty of grouse in North Wales, 'but difficult to get at' – wild weather made the birds unapproachable.

Sir Watkin Wynn has had the Duke O' Aumale and Lord Fielding, among others, at his shooting quarters near Bala, and we heard of daily bags of 20–30 brace. The best sport, however, that has reached our ears, has been on the Nantyr hills, belonging to Col Myddleton Biddulph, MP, who, with Gen Sir J. Michel, Col Madocks, Mr Cornwallis West, and two others, averaged 60–70 brace a day, killing nearly 400 brace in six days. At this rate the Welsh moors will very soon eclipse many of the Scotch shootings, for which fabulous sums are paid, and on which very little is killed.

With increasing competition for let moors, rents escalated and eventually were comparable with those paid by sheep farmers, then at the peak of their prosperity, giving the landlords the best of both worlds. The bubble burst as Australia's wool production got into full stride. Grouse rents continued to rise through the third quarter of the century and many men abandoned sheep, deriving higher incomes from grouse and deer. The economic importance of grouse was established.

'At Break of Day' by Archibald Thorburn, dated 1930 (Courtesy of the Tryon Gallery)

4
Driven to Distraction

*Between 1870 and 1900, grouse-driving became firmly established,
but the pursuit of record bags by a minority repeatedly raised the
question of sportsmanship within the press*

With professional gamekeepers installed on many moors the shepherds could no longer do as they pleased. The grouse-shooters now knew that it was the heather that carried the grouse so the shepherds were prevented from burning it *indiscriminately* on vast tracts of hillside. At first this did not matter because there was lots of young heather where the moors had been burnt. But soon there was no food for the sheep except on those moors where the farmers had acquired both the shooting and grazing rights, and there was no food for the grouse where there was no food for the sheep. On moors where there was no burning the grouse began to die off and at first it was wrongly thought that the culprit was disease rather than starvation. Thus in 1872 and 1873 disaster struck the moors. However, on moors that carried sheep and were burnt regularly, the grouse did not die, so the shooters started to burn the heather systematically, as Lord Dalhousie had been doing in Forfarshire for many years.

Landowners also soon discovered that southern visitors not only wanted to shoot grouse in pleasant, wild surroundings, but also that they wanted to shoot them in large numbers. A particular attraction was that the early opening of the grouse-shooting season on 12 August tied in well with the sportsman's social calendar. Thus it was the common custom of the great landowners and their guests in the last quarter of the nineteenth century to remain on their moors from the glorious opening until well into September, when they would return to their lowland shoots to walk-up a few partridges before the first big, driven partridge days in late September and October, followed by the first of the big pheasant days in late November.

For some of these men large bags were not enough; they also had to be top Gun, bringing down more birds than their friends on as many occasions as possible. But even then this unsporting practice was roundly condemned by most true sportsmen and was not widely condoned. Indeed, the matter had assumed such gravity by the disaster year of 1872, *The Field* felt the need to devote their 24 August leader to the issue:

> The zealous sportsman is in one of his worst moods at this season. His friends with him on the moors would sincerely wish it were lawful to put a log round his neck, to restrain his efforts to have every shot to himself. It is extraordinary how this vice will display itself in persons in other respects incapable of vulgarity or forwardness; and it is as difficult to break them of it as it is to train back to good manners a pointer that has been for a month accustomed to race against his master for possession of a dead bird. Some men are so intolerable in this

MIDLAND RAILWAY.

Entirely Revised and Improved

EXPRESS TRAIN SERVICES ARE NOW IN OPERATION.

SCOTLAND.

Three Fast Morning Expresses, Afternoon Expresses, and Three Evening Expresses in each direction.

LAKE DISTRICT.

Through Expresses to and from London (St. Pancras) and Principal Towns.

YORKSHIRE.

ifteen Expresses in each direction between London (St. Pancras) and Yorkshire.

PEAK OF DERBYSHIRE.

Fast Expresses, London (St. Pancras), and Buxton, Matlock, Manchester, &c.

BREAKFAST CARS.	LUNCHEON CARS.
DINING CARS.	SLEEPING CARS.

JOHN MATHIESON,

Derby, July, 1901.   GENERAL MANAGER.

London & North-Western Railway.

ROYAL MAIL ROUTE

BETWEEN

ENGLAND, IRELAND, AND SCOTLAND.

Through Express Trains are run at frequent intervals between London, Birmingham, Liverpool, Manchester, Preston, the English Lake District, North, South, and Central Wales, Carlisle, Scotland, and Ireland, with connections to and from the manufacturing districts of South Staffordshire, Chester, Holyhead, Bolton, Blackburn, Bradford, Halifax, Leeds, and the manufacturing districts of Yorkshire.

Many of the Express Trains between London and the North call at Willesden Junction, and Special Train Services are in operation between Willesden and Victoria, Willesden and the Crystal Palace and Croydon, Willesden and Kensington (for Waterloo and the London & South Western Railway), Willesden and Southall, connecting with the Lines South of the Thames, and between Willesden, Broad Street, Kew, and Richmond.

Sleeping Saloons are provided by the night trains between London and Liverpool, Manchester, Holyhead, Edinburgh, Glasgow, Stranraer, Perth, and Aberdeen; extra charge 5s. for each berth in addition to the ordinary 1st class fare.

Breakfast, Luncheon, Tea, and Dining Cars are run on the principal trains between London and Liverpool, Manchester, Holyhead, Birmingham, and Wolverhampton.

Corridor Trains with Refreshment and Dining Cars between London and Edinburgh and Glasgow.

Every information as to Trains and Fares can be obtained on application to Mr Robert Turnbull, Superintendent of the Line, Euston Station, London, N.W.

FRED. HARRISON,
General Manager.

Euston Station, London, 1901.

Railway advertisement (1901)

particular that it is simply impossible to keep company and temper with them at the same time. They fire at anything, no matter on what side it gets up. They blaze away at birds in the act of tumbling, or even when they have absolutely touched the heather. They can never load fast enough to exhaust their savage humour for burning powder. And they do not really enjoy themselves, despite their desperate efforts with that intention. They are, as a rule, bad or uncertain Shots . . .

There is, however, a legitimate sort of rivalry and contention in shooting . . . Sportsmen on the moors can easily start, not gambling matches on their skill, but mere challenges in which the reward is repute. Now this also may be done in an objectionable or unobjectionable fashion. It is suspected, for example, that there is occasionally an excessive rivalry *between* moors. One district, say, is shot against another. The point is to make show bags, and to do, in fact, what the hordes of deep-water anglers do for a teapot or a silver watch. Killgillie-crankie must be put down in the papers for as many brought in on the Twelfth as Graygallochgussie, and the respective tenants of both places enter furiously upon as close a war of extermination as decency will permit. And, unfortunately, the line may not be drawn here; the districts in the heat of this struggle may be almost depopulated. The young birds, easiest to bag, and as good to count as any others, go first. Cheepers receive no mercy – they are blown like Sepoys from the mouths of the guns; they are ruthlessly marked down in their short, weak flights, and massacred into pulp. This goes on until the rival sportsmen are warned into prudence by the remarkable scarcity of their game in the middle of September. These bags no doubt serve as excellent advertisements for the shootings, but they can only be regarded by those interested in grouse shooting with complacence when they are not the results of a game of brag, or of cutting down between reckless and ruthless fowlers. We do not assert that this practice, arising from the distinct motive which we have assigned for it, is general. It is perhaps exceptional, but is all the same to be reprehended, and it accounts to us partly for the extraordinary difference that a few days make in the registered shooting of a moor. Even sensible shooters are led into extravagances in this direction. They will not husband the resources that at first seem inexhaustible. They are naturally anxious to figure as expert and deadly contributors to the returns which shortly after the Twelfth are published from the moors . . . We should think far more of large bags at the end of September, at the beginning or middle of October, even if filled by means of driving, which is excusable at that late period. The sportsman who could hold his hand and be content at first with small returns might burst forth on a comparatively clear stage later on, and attract our attention and applause by skill under conditions which do not exist within range of the Twelfth and the opening of the partridge campaign. But this sort of sportsmanlike control is becoming, we suspect, rarer and rarer every day. We want quick, vivid totals in everything, sport included . . . We seem approaching a period when there is danger of grouse shooting being subjected to the ludicrous degradation of that sort of pheasant shooting which is exclusively derived from the nursing of the birds as poultry; or, more ridiculous still, from the circumstance of those agile fowl being purchased full grown the day before the performance, and let loose into the covert from which they are to be flushed as comparatively wild denizens. The grouse, we are grateful to know, cannot be so easily cultivated or manipulated for what might well be termed artificial shooting.

This damning editorial only goes to show that in shooting there is little new under the sun. Today we are still having to grapple with a greedy, unsporting minority who continue to play the numbers game with all forms of quarry and jeopardise the generally good name of shooters everywhere.

The 1872 grouse-shooting season was indeed extraordinary, with enormous numbers of birds killed in the Highlands. These included 7,000 at Dalnadamph by driving, and

10,600 at Glenbuchat over dogs, while individual days produced totals such as 220 brace to one Gun at Grandtully, and 327 brace to three Guns, shooting separately, on Glenquoich.

A decade of regular driving had, by then, brought the Yorkshire moors to their best, and there even more surprising results could be shown. On no less than five Yorkshire moors in that season, over 1,000 brace were killed in a day. At Wemmergill and High Force the season's total reached 17,074 and 15,484 birds respectively, the latter figure the result of nineteen days' driving. The Marquis of Ripon's seven-Gun party bagged 1,006 brace on Dallowgill Moor on the 13th, and on the following day the same group, including crack Shot Earl de Grey, shot a further 630 brace at Harper Hill Moor.

Dallowgill Moor's memorial to one of the greatest Shots of all time

An indication of general attitudes to these exceptional bags is shown by Frederick A. Milbank's letter to *The Field* of 31 August, concerning his Wemmergill Moors:

Sir – In sending you the account of my first three days sport on these moors, I am aware that the amount killed may be open to question and cavil, as last year. I therefore enclose a perfectly correct account of the number of grouse killed by each gentleman, and also the number I myself killed at each drive. I shot with three guns, and only on four occasions during the first day were two birds killed at one shot. The first shot was fired at 8.20, and we left off at eight. Lord Rivers shot only half of the first day, missing four drives, and did not shoot at all the second. A good many birds were picked up the following day, but those only were counted that were actually picked up at the time at each 'stand'. The account sent refers to brace, and not birds. The birds are very fine, and not a single unhealthy one seen.

	Aug 20 Brace	21st Brace	23rd Brace
Mr Fredk Milbank, MP	364	214½	129½
Mr M. W. Vane Milbank	195	144	86
Mr Powlett Milbank	165	73	81
Mr Preston	112	60	75
Lord Rivers	75	–	94½
Collinson	126	112	86½
Total	1,037	603½	552½

After that bumper season, the Yorkshire moors were to hold their own for many years, with consistently high bags, but it was a puzzle that they made no further advance since the only bar to progress seemed to be limited food. It was to be many years before the limits of habitat were even moderately understood.

Despite the increased bags made available, many people were still very much against the whole concept of driving. One of the most influential opponents of the period was Lewis Clement, who was, for many years, shooting and yachting correspondent of *The Field* before he founded *Shooting Times* (then *Wildfowler's Shooting Times and Kennel Gazette*) in 1882. He made the following remarks in 1876 and they were published in his 1877 book *Shooting, Yachting and Sea-fishing Trips*:

Truly the poetry of shooting is going, and going very fast, too . . . Game is now shot with a solemnity that would be in its place at a funeral; it is now performed in the same business-like style, and with that want of fire and enthusiasm that must perforce accompany the necessary operation of fowls' throat-cutting, on the eve of market days, in a well-appointed and well-regulated farmhouse.

Charles Whymper painted this grouse for Charles Dixon's 1900 book Game Birds and Wild Fowl of the British Islands

'Grouse shooting in the Highlands', 1858, painted by Alexander Rolfe

RED GROUSE.
Lagopus scoticus.

Gamekeepers such as Willie Veitch have been the backbone of both grouse-shooting and upland conservation

A loader is essential for first-class driven grouse-shooting

There are no illusions. Game used to be considered with a feeling akin to respect, and this feeling is still lurking within the breasts of some inveterate sportsmen; but our young men of the day have no such feelings. I believe they look upon a pheasant merely as representing a certain amount of shillings and pence, nothing more nor less. Of course it must be so, for when pheasants are reared like chickens, and fattened like pigs, they must needs in time be killed for the market. It is but a speculation. Momentarily speaking, however, the speculation is often a bad one; but then pheasants are fashionable, and what will not a man spend in order to procure that which the world pronounce *de bon ton?*

However, all this is a mere matter of business; it cannot be called sport, and with it we have nothing to do; eventually, no doubt, our shooters will return to the orthodox way of shooting, ie, let the game grow wild, and take the trouble to find out where it lives, and how it is to be found.

A great deal has been said about the every-day increasing necessity for battueing and driving. I admit that for grouse, in certain special cases drives must be resorted to in order to reach the birds, but battueing all coverts I hold not to be a necessary expedient . . .

Born in 1844, Clement had enjoyed the best of most types of shooting throughout Europe, but he was an odd character and admitted to putting business before friends. Thus, in later years, in order to further the interests of his *Shooting Times*, in print, at least, he became a champion of rearing and release and driven shooting. That said, he had an infectious enthusiasm which few subsequent scribes have managed to convey. Take, for example, his account of the Glorious Twelfth, in his above-mentioned book. Clement was awakened by the servant of his host: 'The master is up and getting ready, and breakfast is waiting.' Dawn was just breaking and Clement was dreading the heat in the hottest August since the 1840s.

No Range Rovers for them: they marched off from the squire's house to the moor and on the way Clem shot a rabbit. On the brow of a hill two pointers – Clem's Bang and Jess – were loosed, but the brace of setters kept on a leash. There were three Guns and a lad to help the squire. Clem approached one 'point':

Bang was in a half circle, his chest heaving tremendously, and his great brown eyes turning slowly, from us to the point where his nose told him that the birds were. He never moved, and as Sam trains his dogs to remain on point, and does not induce them to go on when the Guns come up to them, we had to pass him. The moment we did so he turned himself straight, and became as rigid as a marble statue, and up went the lot – nine, all told. The 'old 'un', as Sam called the cock, went on a port tack, and I sent him a Schultze dose that pitched him toes over head, like a heap of rags, into a tuft of heather. With my second I settled a 'towerer', who meant going to the moon seemingly.

Meanwhile, Clem's companions shot three birds.

They shot five birds out of the next covey, of eight.

This time the odd bird belonged to me. I had fired at it as soon as it had risen, and the short range had proved a tickler for my Tolley modified choke-bore, for I missed as clean as could be. Fortunately, however, I had no smoke bothering me, as the Schultze powder produces but very little, so that I was enabled, at once, to place efficiently my second barrel, even though the escaping bird was 60 yards off.

By then it was still only 7.30am and the heat was already being felt!

The cool air of the night had vanished. The mists of the valley were gone, and the heather already began to steam – ie above it, for a foot or two, a thick cloud of hot air seemed to dance all over the moor – and that promised badly for scent and sport.

Thus by noon the dogs 'were quite done, both in limb and nose, in spite of water being given them to drink, and some being thrown over them.' The Guns 'took off every part of our clothing that could possibly be dispensed with, and yet we were literally melting.'

This was in great contrast with the previous year, when 'within a quarter of an hour our waterproof boots were thoroughly filled with water'. But now it was

. . . like walking on a thick, well-matted carpet, and very pleasant it would have been but for the hot weather. Howbeit, the bloom on the heather would have done any artist's heart good to behold, and the ever-changing aspect of the light thrown thereon, as the sun by turns brightened some places, and then threw them into comparative gloom by hiding his blazing face behind a fleeting cloud, was something to be beheld in order to be appreciated.

Their four servants, however, 'cared little for that sort of thing and, really, one could not help pitying them, groaning under the weight of our game and the heat of the sun, and yet they looked vastly interested whenever game turned up.'

Later, golden plovers provided 'the next bit of fun', when the Guns were walking in line. They saw 'a small, grey cloud flying over the moor' and stopped. 'They passed right over us. Our six barrels floored about a score, and two wounded ones were followed and picked up by the under-keeper.'

Eventually the heat was too great to walk any more and they returned to the house.

After luncheon, I went to my bedroom, lay on the bed, and went off to sleep.

At 3 o'clock we started anew, but the heat, if anything had increased, and it will therefore be readily imagined that the 'fagging' was of a most delightful kind. Howbeit, when we stopped work, somewhere near 8 o'clock, we were a tremendous long way from the house, and, owing to the scent having considerably improved within the last two or three hours, we had bagged in regal style right throughout. Our bag for the day, over four dogs, was ninety-three

brace of grouse, besides a score of rabbits, the plovers, a hare, and half-a-dozen snipe which we picked up from sundry marshy hollows.

As regards the grouse, I do not believe we shot more than a dozen, without the dogs had pointed them . . . It was a glorious treat indeed, and may dogs again, for ever, be used in pursuit of sport.

Despite his love of traditional shooting methods, Clement was well aware of scientific advance and the latest thinking. On the 1876 season, which had been good throughout England and Scotland, he commented:

This made ample compensation for the bothers which assailed grouse-shooters on account of the disease within the previous four years; and let us trust that, practically, we have seen the last of that unbounded nuisance. It exists still in some parts, but then it ought to be circumscribed, and stamped out at once if possible; and surely it is within the powers of moor-owners and lessees to get it done, even if the whole of their stock had to be exterminated.

In *The Field* the regular reports from moors, manors and forests were much more extensive than they had been in the 1850s and 1860s, reflecting growth in the sport. In their first 1876 report (19 August), returns were 'chiefly remarkable for the almost total absence of any signs of disease', confirming Clement's observations.

This affords another strong argument in favour of the cycle theory, which explains the periodical return of the pest, on the principle that overstocking necessarily leads to decimation from disease, as soon as a certain stock had been reached, beyond which there is a deficiency in some material needful for ensuring perfect health.

They also reiterated the heat problems of which Clement had written. Their Aberdeenshire correspondent wrote of the 12th:

Among the first consignments to pass through Aberdeen on Saturday was a box from the royal moors on its way to Osborne. Only 26 other boxes and hampers passed through on their way southwards, and this small number may be accounted for by the fact that the 12th fell on Saturday, when sportsmen would not care to have their game lying about railway stations all Sunday. Monday and Tuesday were even warmer than Saturday and sport all over the country has been excellent. About 340 boxes passed through Aberdeen on their way south on Monday, containing about 3,000 birds. At Balmoral the party for the royal moors must have been out early, for a box of 9 brace was forwarded by the forenoon Braemar coach to Ballater.

In Durham, at Scayille Moors, Barnard Castle, belonging to Sir Talbot Clifford Constable, shooting was 'very productive during three days in the old fashion over dogs', with 123 brace, 41 brace and 51 brace, plus hares, rabbits, snipe and plover. 'Count Roven de Louart and Count Chabot of the old regime of France distinguished themselves.'

A decade later, in 1887, sport, according to *Shooting Times*, 'excelled any shooting remembered since 1872'. On 16 December the journal reported:

The grouse were found wonderfully abundant, in fact a trifle too numerous to sell well. Prices this year ruled low. Sixteen shillings a brace was heard of during the first day, but thereafter the supply swamped the market, and from 2s 6d to 3s per brace was all the dealer could afford.

That year saw the publication of Edwin Lester Arnold's book *Bird Life in England*. The chapter on grouse moors and deer forests was written by J. W. Brodie Innes and was, according to *Shooting Times*, 'masterly':

How welcome is the eve of the 12th to those whose fortune it is to have toiled through a long, hot summer amongst city dust for the rest of northern moors.

That night journey itself that takes us northward, with all the luxury of modern travel, is, the first time we make it, an experience the fascination of which never fades. There is the wonderful rush through the fertile Midlands, the chequered landscape under the moonlight, the long gleam of lights of sleeping towns whose names we can only guess at as we fly over the faultless steel roadway, and then the lurid flare of the furnaces down the Vale of Trent. We have had our hot coffee, and taken our cigarettes, and perhaps 'forty winks' in the folds of our thick ulsters, when dawn comes in the east over the deep dells and stone walls of Cumberland; and classic Ribblesdale, that most fascinating valley, holds us before the sun has melted a single dewdrop or thawed the thin white frost that silvers the shadows. What does it matter that we have lost a night's rest, and that we are perchance somewhat travel-stained? The Border is at hand, and beyond it lie heather lands and those grouse we have thought and dreamt of during weary days at work and the dusty crabbed hours of endless sessions. To-night we shall be amongst the hills, and to-morrow we shall breathe again air that is worth inspiring, and look upon some scenes that are a tonic and a sedative – a very lethe of happiness to a hack of dusty civilisation.

Innes also spoke longingly of the old days, when a reasonably stocked moor could be had,

. . . if not actually for the asking, for about the price of a week's shooting in the southern shires today. There was more adventure and more sport . . . and decidedly more of roughing it . . . It was a tour of many changes, from mail-coach to dog-cart, and trap to pony, to reach outlying moors, the shooter and his friends provisioning themselves for a siege.

Men shot '. . . with greater moderation, more pleasure in the shooting, and less in seeing the total of their bags in the next batch of local papers.'

However, he was acutely aware of conflicts within grouseland:

The teaching of our demagogues that moor and mountain belong to the peasant and should be cultivated for and by him alone is difficult to refute, because there is a grain of truth in it. Some 70 per cent of the Highlands cannot and will never be cultivated by any crop that the crofter can afford to rear. Such soil, rock it were almost better to call it, is fit only for grouse and the slow-growing firs and spruces (harbouring capercailzie and black-cock) which give no return for capital for 20 years. As for the remaining percentage of land, much of it is cultivated. If it *will* grow crops and does not, then it ought to. It is on this peg of a little cultivable land uncultivated that agitators hang all their grievances; and landowners would do wisely by taking the ground from under their feet and helping crofters to reclaim that strip of bog they covet, and to build a cot to look after their poor harvest of ragged grain. The shame of the Highlands to-day . . . are the few incorrigible landlords whose views have not broadened with the times, and who would tyrannise in medieval style over a long-headed and thoughtful yeomanry who are germinating new ambitions under the light of better education.

It is such, and the harshnesses of American millionaires, who oust pet lambs from cottagers' paddocks, and depopulate glens to keep a few more head of deer, that endanger our northern shooting and strengthen the hands of demagogues.

This far-sighted author was also aware of the economic benefits of grouse-shooting:

It is the influx of visitors, the trade, and the briskness they bring with them that must be chiefly held to benefit the Highlands, and socially justify the devoting of wide wastes to the muir-fowl. Let it be always remembered, and the evidence is at hand in Government Reports, that the farmers, large and small, of the great English game-rearing shires, turned out to be the warmest supporters of game-rearing and preserving when examined before the Game Laws Committee of the House of Parliament. It is the orators of Manchester allies and politicians of the salubrious slums of Chelsea who object on principle to property in fur or feather.

Poaching remained a major problem and Innes outlined some of the dodges by which grouse were trapped:

Tramps and loafers from the nearest towns set horse-hair nooses in their runs amongst the heather; and, as they often forget where many a springe had been placed, such nooses may remain set until the spring, and take parent birds, with nest adjacent. Again, in autumn, the reapers – always ready for a little work of the kind – stroll out of an evening, under the pleasant yellow harvest moon, and peg down fine nooses atop of the barley shocks. As a result of this sundry grouse are found there, flapping helplessly, head downwards, next morning, before the mists are off the low meadows. A few find their way into rabbit traps, and at least one has been taken in a steel hawk trap, on top of a pole; but of all destructive and objectionable methods, netting of grouse by fixed nets is, perhaps, the worst.

They consist of long lines of fine netting hung on poles, usually by the proprietors of small, narrow allotments facing big moors, where a large head of game is reared. Now, when grouse fly, they rise 10 or 12 feet perpendicularly, and then rush forward at the same height with a velocity which must be seen to be understood, and thus they plunge headlong into the meshes with a force which generally disables them at once. Instead of fair give-and-take, which is the rule amongst neighbouring landowners in matters of game, these daytime poachers take all they can lay hands on, and hardly rear a score of grouse in return.

Much as Innes was concerned about threats to grouse-shooting, he was equally determined to portray the thrill of the sport, and as that is my prime intention, too,

I must include some of his enthusiastic passages. Among these is his description of the last day of the season, when he accepted an invitation from a neighbour:

Looking out the following morning the prospect was wintry enough. All the higher spurs of the ragged neighbouring mountains lay shrouded in snow . . . Truly the hand of winter was coming down upon the land, and in a little time even the few still occupied shooting lodges would be bare and empty of their summer migrants.

Breakfast over, myself and J climbed into the waiting dog-cart . . . and tucking in the comfortable rugs, for an autumn morning in the Highlands before the sun is well over the hill-tops is none too warm, J picked up the ribbons, flicked the sleek-coated chestnut, and away he went down the drive, our cigars aglow, and minds full of pleasant anticipation.

Half an hour's sharp trotting brought us to the beginning of the long avenue which led to our entertainer's noble mansion.

After hearty but hurried introductions, for the hour was late, they followed the headkeeper down a winding path into the valley below the house:

The morning was lovely, cold and clear as could be wished, while our 'fighting line', winding through a deep forest of firs, was really a picturesque sight. First went the keeper in his national dress, a man of strength and stature, and an awe to all the poachers far or near; then our host, P, discussing the merits of a new trout fly with an Assam tea planter, R, whose gun, carried over his shoulder, had recently been dealing out death and destruction to the snipe on the plains of India. On their heels came our host's son talking to 'Uncle P', and two cousins, both in Athole tartans. These, myself, J, and one other young laird made up the party. We wound down the narrow path in single file, the occasional gleams of sunshine breaking into the cool shade of forest to glitter on our gun barrels. We chatted and laughed until, having dipped into a lovely glen, thick with amber fern and silver birches, we crossed a rocky torrent bed, scaled the opposite bank, and soon found ourselves by a thatched cottage, where keepers with numerous dogs in lash awaited our arrival. Now chaff and fun had to be given up, for we were about to begin the serious business of the day. Our host led us out of the wood, across a patch of rocky ground, through a gap in a stone wall, and there we were on the breezy hillside, knee deep in heather, breathing such nectar as dwellers in towns never dream of, with in front a limitless expanse of mountain and moorland undisturbed as far as the eye could see by a trace of civilization . . .

Overleaf: 'End of the Season' by Archibald Thorburn (Courtesy of the Tryon Gallery)

Archibald Thorburn 1909

Soon they were in their first positions, chilled by the winds blowing across the snow-fields, bringing to their ears the far away bleat of mountain sheep, or the melancholy whistle of a plover, whose sharp eyes already saw the advancing beaters:

But the sun was warm overhead and our pipes smoked fragrantly. Presently a distant shout comes down to us, and the Guns all down the line are to be seen directly on the *qui vive*; cartridges are hastily arranged, caps securely 'crammed' down on their wearers' heads, and all eyes are directed over the wall to get a wider view of the plain in front; and soon the grouse come in sight on the far left of the line, giving the last man one chance, and his gun immediately breaks the silence of the hills, the white puff of smoke sailing away over the heather to leeward . . .

Thus the sport continued, with varying success and some over-enthusiasm among the younger members of the party, till a little past midday, when they broke for lunch, provided by their host's daughter in:

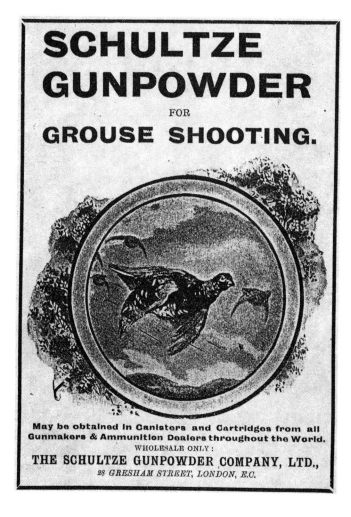

. . . a sheltered nook, cut deep through the moor by the ceaseless labours of a sparkling streamlet . . . It is by no means the worst part of the day; the provender is ample and varied, cold grouse pies, flanked by such salads as must surely have grown in celestial kitchen gardens, a sirloin of the finest stalled beef, pastry of fairy lightness, unimpeachable drink that, when accepted in foaming tankards from the fair fingers of our fascinating Hebe, becomes quite ambrosial. We linger, too, over the choice cheroots which our host passes round after the meal; thus careless of time until the edges of the purple shadows creeping up the opposite hillside warn us that autumn days are all too short for much idleness, so we see the 'mem sahib' to her pony carriage in the neighbouring lane and then are soon hard at work once more.

A year after Arnold's book was published, came news of the biggest individual bag of grouse on record. On 30 August, 1888, Lord Walsingham killed 1,070 grouse to his own gun, on Blubberhouse Moor in Yorkshire, easily beating his 1872 record. With forty beaters in two teams, the first drive started at 5.12am and the last, the 20th, finished at 6.45pm, following which Walsingham rounded the day off by walking home for a further fourteen birds. The details of the drives were:

	Time		Minutes	Birds killed
	From	To		
1	5.12	5.45	33	49
2	5.57	6.15	18	64
3	6.34	6.50	16	59
4	7.10	7.28	18	79
5	7.46	8.10	24	71
6	8.35	8.53	18	58
7	9.15	9.34	19	56
8	10.02	10.22	20	53
9	10.37	10.57	20	42
10	11.24	11.40	16	61
11	12.11	12.30	19	16
12	12.45	1.15	30	21
13	1.25	1.50	25	32
14	2.14	2.35	21	91
15	2.45	3.13	28	39
16	3.35	3.56	21	93
17	4.15	4.35	20	52
18	5.01	5.25	24	33
19	5.49	6.10	21	23
20	6.25	6.45	20	30
Walk	7.00	7.30	30	14
		Killed in drives		1,022
		Killed in walk		14
		Pick-up		34
		TOTAL		1,070

Walsingham used four central-fire, breechloading Purdey black-powder hammer-guns and two loaders, and nearly half the time was spent in waiting for the beaters or in picking-up. Only once during the day were three birds killed with one shot (the only three in view at the moment, as it happened), and three times two birds were killed at one shot, each time intentionally. A fairly strong west wind was blowing, which made the birds flying downwind fine sporting shots. The time of the drives was usually taken from the second shot because a straggling bird frequently causes the first shot to be fired long before the main body of birds arrives, but it was found that this was not so often the case on this occasion as had been expected.

In a letter giving details of the day to his friend Sir Ralph Payne-Gallwey, Walsingham said he fired 'just about 1,500' shots '. . . after deducting 40 for signal shots'. He added: 'You know I fire long shots and counting many second barrels to birds hit by the first but seeming to require another pellet this is not so bad as it looks. I am quite sure all the same that I was not in my best form – the cartridges were *not good* at all.' He worked out his average at about 2⅓ birds per minute actual shooting.

In another letter, in the *Morning Post* of 8 September, Walsingham wrote:

Yesterday morning I took a walk to see what were left. Two keepers, with a pony and saddle-bags, accompanied myself and my loader – of course without setters or pointers. It was a quarter to one before I set foot on the moor, and during the day I killed 26 brace. This a few years ago would have been regarded as a very large bag to make over dogs on the 12th of August, and, as a fact, the largest bag ever made here by one Gun without driving has been 42½ brace. It is remarkable that such a bag as 26 brace should now be possible after a cold, wet breeding season, which killed off a vast proportion of young birds, and after the actual stock has already been reduced by 1,786 on a total area of only 2,221 acres.

Walsingham was so egotistic he immediately wrote correcting any editor who had even the smallest detail wrong concerning his big day. Less enthusiastic observers said the birds were driven backwards and forwards on the hourglass-shaped moor, and passers-by recorded that grouse lay by the road too tired to move. His half-brother, John de Grey, who succeeded him, later wrote: 'The stone passages of the farmhouse where we were staying were stacked with grouse three and four feet deep. For a fortnight the place was swarming with the lice left behind.' And it was said that Walsingham went for the record because the King had refused his invitation and friends said his moor was 'too little'.

In the book *Shooting – Moor and Marsh*, which he wrote with Sir Ralph Payne-Gallwey, Walsingham went to great lengths to justify both driven shooting and his record day. Indeed, much of his comment makes good sense, but the fact remains that even then deliberate record-seeking involving quarry birds and mammals was a questionable practice and today it must be despised by anyone who ventures to call himself a sportsman.

However, there were to be many more big bags and driving was firmly established

Pointers by George Earl (Courtesy of the Tryon Gallery)

as the backbone of the sport of grouse-shooting. As the nineteenth century drew to a close, the position was summarised in *The Field* for 13 August, 1898:

> The 'dog' man may affect to sneer at his brother the 'driver', but whilst granting the fact that grouse-shooting over dogs is an exhilarating pastime, it cannot be denied that the sport of driving fascinates even more strongly all those who take to it. It may be that the sportsman's appreciation increases in proportion with the difficulties which beset him; for it is equally understandable that the shooting of driven grouse or partridges taxes the skill of the gunner to a greater extent than any other form of sport with the shotgun. Then, too, it is possible that even the bitterest opponents of the modern system will concede that driving exercises a certain beneficent influence on a moor. Anyhow, it is certain that much heavier bags are now secured by driving than were ever made by 'dogging' under the most favourable conditions, and thus the annual return for some moors has been very much increased, perhaps doubled. The marvellous shooting of the late Sir F. A. Millbank on Wemmergill, and of Lord Walsingham on

Blubberhouse Moors, first opened out to sportsmen the great possibilities of the system of driving grouse. Since then truly remarkable bags have been made, and as proof that the moors are not in any way drained beyond recuperation by such heavy shooting it may be mentioned that Lord Westbury and a party of 8 Guns have since killed 2,234 grouse in a single day on the Wemmergill Moors. Then, too, on Mr Rimington-Wilson's Broomhead Moor 2,626 birds have been killed in 6½ hours shooting. Again, more recently, the same moor yielded 2,648 grouse in one day to nine Guns; whilst – and this perhaps, is more remarkable still – on the same ground two days later no less than 1,603 grouse were killed. This conclusively proves what may be accomplished by driving under the most favourable conditions. But, of course, it goes without saying that bags such as these are possible only to first-rate Shots.

The last sentence made a particularly important point because driven grouse-shooting is undoubtedly very difficult. How often today we see rich novices totally bewildered by the first-class sport they have managed to buy their way into. Even Guns who have been successful with other quarry, such as pheasants, generally find initial difficulty in getting to grips with the King of Gamebirds.

But questions of management and sportsmanship were not the only problems which the sport would take into the twentieth century. In particular there was the apparent selfishness involved in devoting such a massive acreage to the preservation of a single species to provide sport for a privileged minority. In 1889 James Bryce's Access to Mountains Bill had been rejected for a second time, on the representation of grouse-moor owners. 'The scenery of our country has been filched away from us just when we have begun to desire it more than ever before,' Bryce told Parliament. He maintained that his Bill never had a chance because the pursuit of grouse had become '. . . a solemnity of the utmost importance'. How surprised he would be to learn that the problem remains largely unresolved a century later.

5

Sporting Wars

From the Boer War to the Great War, servicemen everywhere were sustained by sporting memories and grouse-shooters soldiered on through thick and thin

Tis a fine opening day!
To the moors will away
all the World and his wife and his kin,
over bents, hags and bogs,
with drivers and dogs
keen as Coleman's best brand to begin.
Every butt with new turfs is OK,
fingers itch to be blazing away.
With the grouse in the ling
wild and strong on the wing,
we must all go a-shooting today!

W. Carter Platts, 1905

A grouse moor with heather in full bloom must have been among the most nostalgic visions of home for so many soldiers fighting for Queen and Empire in far-flung corners of the world at the turn of the century. Indeed, there is nothing better than the horrors of war to focus the mind on so-called true values. Thus it was not surprising that on 3 August, 1901 the *Shooting Times & British Sportsman* began thus:

We hear that shootings have been taken up exceptionally well this season, probably due to the rosy prospects of sport, and also to the return of many sportsmen who were away all last season with the Army in South Africa. Those who have left the renting of shoots until a late hour will, we fear, have to put up with what they can get, and even then will probably have to pay stiff prices for inferior shoots. Every year shoots become more expensive, and more difficult to obtain within a reasonable distance of town. The large number of American sportsmen who come over here with unlimited cash are to some extent responsible for the rise in prices. It is the fashion in England to shoot grouse in August, and grouse our Yankee cousins will have at any cost.

Such hypocrisy continues to this day, with many British sportsmen secretly resenting the invasion from across the 'Pond' but at the same time stressing that the rural economy of northern Britain is dependent on grouse-shooting revenue.

On a more practical note, *Shooting Times* reported:

Soon kind friends will be sending presents of grouse all over the country. Many of these will be lost, or, rather, stolen in transit, and numbers of shooting men will wonder at never receiving any acknowledgement from their friends that they have received the leash of grouse, which were tied together by the necks and duly despatched with a visiting card carrying the compliments of the sender . . . Last season so many parcels of game were lost that an enquiry was held by some of the head officials of the leading railway companies . . . We recommend that shooting men advise their friends that game is being forwarded.

Grouse were abundant that year and this aggravated the problem of falling prices, as reported in *Shooting Times* on 17 August:

A noteworthy feature of this Twelfth was that birds were not displayed in gamedealers' shops until the afternoon, and that the prices were by no means so high as they usually are; plenty of birds could be obtained at 10s, and even 8s per brace. Whether the cold storage warehouses, which are, by the way, greatly on the increase, affect the prices of the birds we know not, but the fact remains that the large quantities of grouse that had been stored away for many months in the ice houses were brought to light on this Twelfth and were readily disposed of to hotels and restaurants.

However, a large number of these birds were obviously not shot by driving. The same issue of *Shooting Times* stated:

With very few exceptions all the shooting at the beginning of the season is done over dogs, and in spite of what we hear about the disappearance of pointers and setters, they are, we hear, more in evidence than ever this season. We certainly think that the use of good dogs makes the sport far more attractive at the beginning of the season. Of course later on, when the birds become wilder, there is no alternative but driving.

In the following week the journal saw fit to issue the customary warning about the need to be fit for shooting over dogs, especially when it is hot early in the season:

. . . about as trying an ordeal as one could undergo – so far as the average untrained individual is concerned. Before the first two hours are over the untrained shooter is wringing with perspiration, and as sorry an individual as you could wish to see. Heart-beat and respiration are at an abnormal rapidity; in fact, he is so out of breath it is painful to watch him pant laboriously up the hillside. His heart is thumping tumultuously against his chest walls; then, to cap all, he drinks greedily from the first spring he comes to, and it is all up with him, for the latter indiscretion brings about a temporary 'broken winded' condition from which he will not recover for the rest of the day . . . Woeful misses are the melancholy result . . . He might as well go home, have a bath and devote the

rest of the day to nap or billiards. If a man wants to walk and shoot well he should go in for a little training, such as cycling or walking, instead of lolling away in his yacht or on the Continent. He should also diet a bit, and not indulge in heavy suppers, strong cigars and alcohol for at least a fortnight before he steps into the heather.

Again, there is little new under the sun; so many of us are determined to 'burn the candle at both ends'.

The 1901 season certainly lived up to expectations. Among the most exceptional bags was 420 brace on only 1,000 acres – on Carron Moor. Also at the end of August, the Mackintosh of Mackintosh broke the record for a day's grouse driving in Scotland: he and his friends killed over 900 brace on the Moy Hall Moors in Inverness-shire. In London on 4 September young grouse were selling for 4s 6d to 5s a brace and old birds 2s 2d to 2s 4d a brace. During just one week in August a gamedealer in Richmond, Yorkshire, sent away no fewer than 17,352 grouse, the price ranging as low as 2s a brace.

Poaching continued to trouble the moors, and on 2 November *Shooting Times* described another of the dodges adopted by the old Yorkshire and Scottish thieves, that of the peat larder:

> Lots of grouse that appear in the markets on the Twelfth are poached birds, which have been killed perhaps some weeks previously. The poacher has no cold storage rooms, so he proceeds to construct a cupboard to hold his poached game until the close season ends. After killing a few brace of good birds he cuts a fair-sized hole in a dry stratum of peat, which is always found on the moors, and in the hole so made he deposits the birds, and carefully closes the entrance with blocks of dry peat. In this larder the birds can be left for a considerable time without decay, as the dry peat acts as a capital preservative.

Among the most remarkable bags of this period, was that of 2,748, made on one day in August, 1904, on Mr R. H. Rimington-Wilson's Broomhead Moor, only 8 miles from 'grimy' Sheffield. This caused considerable comment in the American press, over-zealous but misinformed writers complaining of English '. . . sportsmen

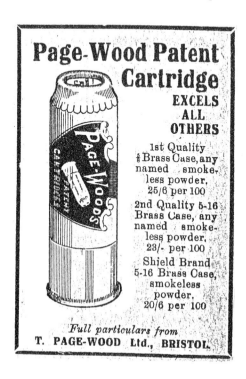

with a crude and brutal mentality butchering thousands of tame birds'. They also inferred that the Guns were 'sitting in blinds'. Now, of course, Americans are the greatest supporters of first-class British grouse-shooting.

Broomhead, in fact, was a highly progressive, showpiece shoot, where bags approaching the record had already been made since the 1890s, yet the moor covered just 4,000 acres and in 1858 the record day produced just eighty-two birds. And on 27 August, 1913 nine Guns were to bag 2,843. Often only two days were shot, and their great success was in virtual elimination of disease through fine moor management and stock control. Also, whereas Walsingham used twenty short drives to achieve his record personal bag at Blubberhouses, six long drives were the daily limit for Wilson.

A former Wilson of Broomhead is said to have been the first man to shoot a grouse on the wing, in the middle of the seventeenth century. I cannot imagine what he would have thought of life in the latter part of the twentieth century, when his celebrated moor's nearness to large towns has made it handy for 'rent-a-mob' and mass trespass.

By the end of Edward VII's reign, the letting of grouse-moors was still much affected by the course of parliamentary business. A good letting season hung on whether Parliament ceased from its sessional labours in time for celebration of the day of St Grouse. But 'this event is generally prophetically known some time in advance,' wrote George Malcolm in *Grouse and Grouse Moors* (1910).

> Autumn sessions of Parliament are abhorred by Highland lairds and other owners of grouse moors. In this aspect of the matter it may be said that the unprecedentedly prolonged session of 1909 was one of the most disastrous on record, many of the choicest and most highly rented shootings having either been without tenants at all or let at seriously reduced rents.

This, of course, had serious economic effects on the various neighbourhoods. He continued:

> In Scotland shootings are not only more extensive and valuable, but receive more attention as a calculated source of income than in the sister countries. It is computed that there are, of all clases, 3,354 shootings in Scotland which are either regularly let or shot over by their owners; of these 3,157 are grouse and general shootings, and 197 are deer forests, which also contain a certain number of grouse and other game. If the average rent of a Scottish grouse moor and other shootings, exclusive of deer forests, be taken at £250, the *cumulo* annual rental will be £789,250.

Then, as now, shoot tenants expected value for money and there was plenty of 'new' cash about for suitable support services. George Malcolm again:

> Your first-class sporting tenant – English or American; never Scottish or Irish, and seldom any of the continental peoples – gives liberally for his privileges, and

exacts liberal advantages besides the bare right to shoot. The lodge must be commodious – furnished, and kept almost to the standard of metropolitan modern life. Electric lighting, garage for motor-cars, facilities for yachting and salmon fishing where practicable, and many other luxuries, or, as some would say, superfluities, are now looked upon as indispensable; while every department of the internal economy of the house, especially the culinary arrangements, must be in quite first-rate order and capacity.

Gone were the days when the annual invasion of the Highlands was 'chiefly by means of lumbering, heavy old family carriages', with 'processions of antique vehicles, now entirely obsolete, drawn by relays of hired horses with postillions, for weeks on the dusty highways, slowly threading their way . . .' Now, according to Stuart Wortley, you could kill a right-and-left of Perthshire grouse just sixteen hours from the time you were driving through Bloomsbury on the Scotch Mail, a journey which would have taken eight days fifty years beforehand.

Then, in 1911, came a milestone in the history of grouse-shooting, with the publication of *The Grouse in Health and Disease*, by E. Wilson, R. T. Leiper and A. Shipley, edited by Lord Lovat. Earlier studies had merely classified birds as harmful or beneficial, solely on the basis of their diet, but this new work laid the foundations of modern ecology. It heralded the scientific study of gamebirds and elevated game biology to a highly respected place in the wider field of wildlife conservation and management.

Moors in northern England were highly sought after at this time, the best in Yorkshire being let for about £1 a brace, even without a house. However, rents were as high in the most favoured parts of Scotland, and even in out-of-the-way places 15s a brace was easily obtained. One person who seemed to get all the shooting he wanted for minimal outlay was the King. On the Twelfth he was the guest of the Marquis of Ripon at Studley Royal, where six Guns bagged 570 brace on the famous Dallowgill Moor in Nidderdale. Other guests were the Earl and Countess of Pembroke, the Earl of Durham and Lady Anne Lambton, Lady Juliet Duff, the Marquis de Soveral, Lord Herbert Vane-Tempest, Sir Reginald Lister, Mrs Sneyd and Miss Muriel Wilson.

His Majesty – 'a rattling fine Shot', according to *Shooting Times* – would take in two more brief shoots in the Highlands before proceeding to Balmoral, but he would visit 'one or two country houses in the Midlands and East Anglia from the end of October onwards, when covert shooting is in progress, apart from the dates provisionally reserved for Castle Rising and Windsor Forest.'

On 19 August, *Shooting Times* reported:

The King is now renewing acquaintance with the Duke of Devonshire's famous and extensive Wharfedale Moors, which, from the frequency with which they have been shot over by his majesty and the late King Edward, have come to be regarded almost as royal moors – and they deserve it.

Here King George is able to throw off the burdens of state and 'take to the woods', as it were, for the Duke of Devonshire's shooting lodge, Bolton Hall, is

The 9th Duke of Devonshire at the butts, c1909 (Royal Archives, Windsor)

far too modest in the matter of its accommodation for the entertainment of royalty with its war-paint on.

Breakfast is taken about nine, after which, while the matutinal pipe is in full blast, the chat is of the day's prospects, and lots are drawn for the butts, the royal visitor taking his sporting chance with the other Guns. Then the shooting ponies or motors are brought round and the procession starts for the moors. For many years it has been the custom to open the season on Hazlewood Moor, which has yielded the record bag for the opening day on the Duke's moors of 548 brace. Hazlewood occupies the same heather-clad ridge as its neighbouring moor, Blubberhouses, where Lord Walsingham made his record bag for one Gun, and lies on the north side of the River Wharfe, above the lovely ravine known to the tourist as the Valley of Desolation. High upon the moor is a lone shooting box, known as Rogan Hall, where, joined by the ladies from the Hall, luncheon is taken. Three drives usually occupy the time before lunch, and four are indulged

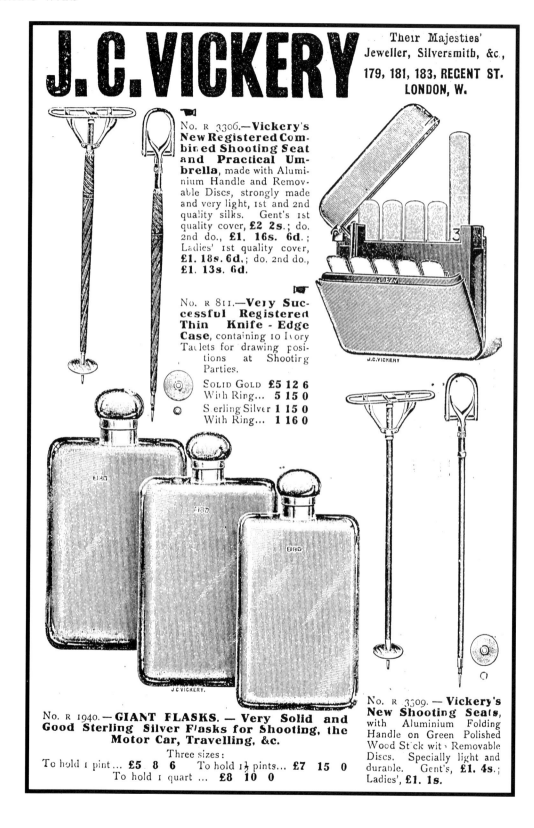

J. C. VICKERY

Their Majesties' Jeweller, Silversmith, &c.,

179, 181, 183, REGENT ST. LONDON, W.

No. R 3306.—**Vickery's New Registered Combined Shooting Seat and Practical Umbrella**, made with Aluminium Handle and Removable Discs, strongly made and very light, 1st and 2nd quality silks. Gent's 1st quality cover, **£2 2s.**; do. 2nd do., **£1. 16s. 6d.**; Ladies' 1st quality cover, **£1. 18s. 6d.**; do. 2nd do., **£1. 13s. 6d.**

No. R 811.—**Very Successful Registered Thin Knife - Edge Case**, containing 10 Ivory Tablets for drawing positions at Shooting Parties.

SOLID GOLD	£5 12 6
With Ring...	5 15 0
Sterling Silver	1 15 0
With Ring...	1 16 0

No. R 1940. — **GIANT FLASKS. — Very Solid and Good Sterling Silver Flasks for Shooting, the Motor Car, Travelling, &c.**

Three sizes :
To hold 1 pint ... **£5 8 6**   To hold 1½ pints... **£7 15 0**
To hold 1 quart ... **£8 10 0**

No. R 3509. — **Vickery's New Shooting Seats**, with Aluminium Folding Handle on Green Polished Wood Stick with Removable Discs. Specially light and durable. Gent's, **£1. 4s.**; Ladies', **£1. 1s.**

in afterwards. Such a delightful dose of the simple life must come as a blessed relief to His Majesty after all the pomp and pageantry of Coronation.

One of His Majesty's other so-called 'brief shoots' was on the Moy Hall moors, as the guest of The McIntosh. Over 3½ days, King George shared butts with The McIntosh, the Marquis of Tullibardine, Lord Lovat, Sir Charles Cust, the Marquis of Stafford, Lieut-Col Ponsonby, Captain Fawcett, and Angus McIntosh of McIntosh. The bag was 460 brace on 22 August, 480 brace on the 23rd, 324 brace on the 24th, and 136 brace in a few hours on the 25th – a total of 1,400 brace. 'Driving was resorted to, and birds were wild and strong.'

In this era, it was also the custom for the leading journals to give extensive details of shoot lettings, among which we discover that Sir Oswald Mosley took Keiss Castle in Caithness-shire for the 1911 season.

Not surprisingly, Ireland was less well supported by English Guns. Apart from the fact it was less accessible, its reputation was mixed. First there was the question of butts, as reported in *Shooting Times*:

We have noticed that butts on Irish moors are generally less conspicuous than elsewhere. Irish workmen are not blessed with the faculty of neatness, and they merely jumble together the sods when they build a butt. The Scotch are given to paring the sods, etc, and although they erect an infinitely better and more substantial butt, it has not the natural appearance presented by the result of Irish handicraft. Again, the moist climate of Ireland keeps the heather and other herbage alive on the sods comprising the butt, and it is therefore in better keeping with the surroundings.

Then there was the fact that not all Irish moorland was pleasing to the eye of the sportsman:

Grouse-shooting on the Irish mountains, such as are to be found in Connemara, Wicklow, Donegal, and Limerick, is pleasing because of the lovely scenery on every side, but for sheer dreariness of outlook commend me to the sport on the flat bogs of King's Co, Westmeath, etc, and all through the Bog of Allen. Grouse are fairly plentiful there, but there is little satisfaction to be derived from staring out of a butt over a bog as flat as a billiard-table. It is extremely difficult to conceal butts there.

Not surprisingly, World War I brought many problems for grouse-shooting. For a start, with so many men away at the front, beaters were very scarce. On 7 August, 1915, *Shooting Times* reported:

Where shooting is indulged in, it will be mostly walking-up. Where troops are stationed, the officers will probably be asked to take a hand, and Tommies who can get leave might like to assist by driving the moors. Useful exercise with relaxation from the daily round would be good for all, whilst the bag would come in useful for the invalids. The King is setting an excellent example. He has given instructions that the necessary thinning-out of the birds shall take place directly the season opens, and, after some of the birds have been reserved for the royal table, the others are to be distributed among the naval and military hospitals.

With the smallest number of Guns for fifty years, the keepers had to consider methods of reducing an exceptionally large grouse stock, to control disease. As a result, Lord Lovat managed to get a Bill through the Lords authorising the shooting of grouse from 5 August. But there was a great deal of controversy over this and many people saw the move merely as a means to ensure a full share of enjoyment for those for whom the war gave less spare time. Not surprisingly, the Commons rejected the Bill, amid shouts of 'We want to shoot Germans, not grouse.' However, the measure was accepted later in the war.

Bidding was poor at the London dog sales, despite the estimated 3 million grouse waiting to be shot, and generally there was little enthusiasm for sport. Sporting agents had to offer moors at half their usual rentals or less. And, surprise, surprise, *Shooting Times* reported that 'numbers of ladies have taken moors . . . probably as the result of confidence by practice at miniature rifle-ranges, where some fair shooters have achieved great reputations as first-class markswomen.'

The possibility of allowing game-shooting on Sundays was mooted, but abandoned because the nation did not realise how long the war would go on for and it was not considered worthwhile to pass the necessary Act of Parliament.

Judging by the prices soon after the Twelfth, there was no shortage of grouse. Young birds sold at 2s 6d–3s a brace and old ones 1s 4d–2s a brace. However, not nearly enough birds were being killed by shooting and sportsmen called for consideration of other methods. In response, and reluctantly because they considered it unsporting, *Shooting Times* gave details of grouse-netting.

The men who took grouse alive by means of nets were usually small hill-farmers whose land joined or in some cases ran right into a grouse moor or moors. When a large pasture field thus divides the grouse ground, a line of nets set up in the said pasture will take enormous toll of the birds as they cross from one part of the moor to another. Naturally, the moor-owners 'had it in' for these netters; but, the latter being on their own ground and properly licensed, the law was powerless to touch them. In some instances the moor-owners bought them out; but, as this usually cost quite a pile of money, it was not always feasible. Other proprietors beat them at their own game by netting against them, and this led to 'ructions' in certain districts.

But by 1915, wholesale netting had declined. Each net was 30ft long and 7–8ft high, depending on the nature of the ground and the height at which the birds flew in particular places. Some were as low as 4ft. The instant birds flew into the fine twine meshes the net parted from the posts and enveloped the captives in a hopeless tangle.

Militol was a popular boot preservative in the early 1920s

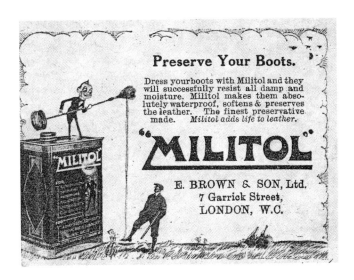

George, Prince of Wales, and companion (note the hammergun) at the butts c1909 (Royal Archives, Windsor)

Many of the birds suffered broken wings and legs and were sold immediately for the table, to middlemen at 15s a brace. Uninjured birds were often kept in a barn or outhouse and fed until the 'fence' could take them.

An alternative method involved laying the nets and posts flat on the ground, as the birds were attracted to feed on such rough patches. But once in the nets they lost their heads completely and there was no chance of escape. And very early in the season, where birds lie well to dogs, it was possible to drag-net the coveys. When the pointer came to a stand, the men made a detour to draw the net downwind towards him, the silk meshes often enveloping the entire family.

As the war continued, determined sportsmen found many ways to improve their situation. For example (*Shooting Times*, 3 August, 1918): 'A small shelf on which to lay cartridges ready for use is a great advantage in these days when loaders are difficult to get, and many men who previously used a pair of guns now use only one.'

The same issue of the magazine also addressed the problem of inexperienced as well as insufficient beaters:

Owing to the scarcity of labour, boys, and even girls, may have to be employed, and in this case shooting may have to be carried on chiefly on a Saturday – a bad day as birds then have to be kept till the following Monday before an opportunity arises of getting them to market. On many moors boys have been selected for the most important positions – as 'props' or 'flankers' – and the result is usually disastrous. The men best acquainted with the moor and the flight of the birds should be placed in these positions, as the waving of a flag at an inopportune moment will deflect the birds from the line of butts and may completely spoil the whole drive. On no account should inexperienced boys or men be used as 'props'.

The cartridge supply did not seem to pose much of a problem, but the shortage of petrol certainly did as the Petrol Control Board would not release petrol solely for use in getting to and from shoots:

In most moorland districts a long drive is necessary, and in the absence of horsed vehicles, which at present are almost unobtainable, very great difficulty will be caused to shooting men. As most of the Guns are men over military age they are unable to walk the long distances that younger men might undertake with impunity.

Game prices were fixed by the Food Controller. Grouse and blackgame were not to exceed 2s 6d to the retailer and 5s 6d to the consumer. The Ministry of Food also ordered that: 'The person owning or taking a shooting is responsible for detaching and keeping the appropriate coupons for game killed on his shooting and consumed in his own household.' For 'self-suppliers' the grouse quota was one coupon for each four birds, and for 'direct supplies' one coupon for each two birds. The quota varied with other quarry and the system was subject to considerable abuse and ridicule.

In the end, the 1915 season was an outstanding success for many moors. The highlight was the record bag of 2,929 grouse which the Earl of Sefton and seven other Guns made on the Littledale and Abbeystead moors in Lancashire, on 12 August. That year the Earl's shoot yielded 17,078 grouse on some 17,000 acres.

Continuing interest in the sport was fostered by a steady stream of books, not the least being Eric Parker's *Shooting Days* (1918), in which he wrote of the Twelfth:

Alone, and above the rest, as every boy's must be, are my first two grouse. They are not a right-and-left, for they rose separately, but they were birds of the same covey, and two barrels were all they needed, which seemed to me in that hour a deed incredible. When the first fell – but do I not see this day the dark peat, the rim of heather, the crumpled form stock-still in mid-air? When the second fell, even then I remained silent; I did not stride to get the prizes into my hands: I heard, as if it were happening to someone else, an order given to pick up those two birds; I saw them picked up, the dog passed me and I touched neither of them. The line of Guns moved on, as if nothing unparalleled in the cosmic scheme had occurred.

Such nostalgic accounts helped many servicemen through the hostilities. Where others carried the Bible or Shakespeare to boost flagging spirits at the Front, game-shooting enthusiasts treasured the words of great sportsmen and a vision of Britain blooming with heather.

6

Fighting Spirit

*After World War I, grouse-shooters scarcely had a chance to consider
increasing comforts before Hitler plunged them into further melancholia*

With the return of peace, the ascendancy of grouse-shooting continued, spearheaded
by the example of George V. However, a legacy of problems remained, especially
concerning the control of vermin, which had proliferated while most keepers were
away on the Continent. As a result, a number of pest-control clubs were formed and,
with increasing interest in wildlife, these were often accused of being over-zealous.

One such body was the Argyllshire Vermin Club, which, stated *The Field* in 1922,
was

> . . . accused of wanton destruction of interesting and beautiful wildlife in the
> form of peregrines, eagles, and buzzards. But it was pointed out on behalf of the
> club that whatever may have been the case before the war, or whatever may be
> the condition elsewhere, in Argyllshire the balance of wildlife had been so
> seriously disturbed that the buzzard, to take only one instance, had become a
> pest; and when birds, however handsome, destroy the living of human beings,
> which was the case with the owners and gamekeepers of Argyllshire moors, who
> saw their income and their wages disappear with the grouse, there is only one
> possible outcome.

Generally though, it was a time to forget war and for shooters to avail themselves
of every new facility. For example, in 1922:

> The exodus to the north for the grouse-shooting season has received the most
> careful consideration of the London and North-Western Railway Company, who
> are this year offering a new feature in connection with their renowned special
> sleeping-car service. Hitherto passengers for the Highlands leaving Euston at
> 7.30pm have found that this departure time necessitated their taking an early
> evening meal in town. With a view to eliminating this disadvantage, the
> company have introduced a dining-car on this train.

And not to be outdone, the Great Northern Railway Company arranged for trains on
the east coast route, from London to Scotland, 'to be augmented as necessary to meet
the expected heavy demand for accommodation. For those preferring to travel by
daylight, luncheon-car expresses will leave King's Cross at 9.50am.'

By the mid-twenties, few sportsmen kept their own kennel of dogs, and it had
become the custom to hire mainly pointers and setters from professional trainers, at

Profiteerer: "What with the rent of the shoot, hire of beaters, and cost of cartridges, these b—— birds have cost me at least thirty bob each."

Visitor: "What a mercy we didn't kill any more of them."

Cartoon (1920)

about £10 each. Understandably, most trainers were given to over-estimate the number needed, such dogs to be sent to the moor by 20 July so that the keeper could get to know their characters and qualities and get them into good, hard condition.

New shooters, too, were constantly reminded of the need to be prepared, and not just bodily. As *Shooting times* commented in 1928:

> There are innumerable advantages to be derived from an afternoon at a shooting school, especially for the busy city man. It is the perfect tonic for tired limbs and jaded nerves, and one also gets the coaching and advice of experts. It is a very good thing indeed to have one's style overhauled.

In response to the constant re-examination of shooting-season dates, which is a favourite pastime of sportsmen to this day, the magazine also offered an explanation of why 12 August should have been selected as the day on which grouse-shooting begins:

By the 13th of George III, c.55, s.2, it was enacted that no person should kill, buy, sell, or have in his possession any grouse between the 10th day of December and the 12th day of August in any year under heavy penalties. However, this does not explain the reason for the Twelfth, and the probability is that the Act merely confirmed an already existing law or custom. Investigation would probably show that the date was originally August 1, Old Style. As is well known, the old calendar had by 1752 got 11 days ahead of solar time, and these days were omitted in that year in order, so to speak, to allow the sun to catch up, September 3 being called September 14. In the following year, 1753, no doubt sportsmen realised that August 1 fell 11 days earlier under the New Style than it had done before, corresponding, in fact, to July 21, Old Style. Hence their adhesion to August 1, Old Style, equivalent to August 12, New Style, as the proper season to begin shooting.

Whatever the season, there was the need to dress correctly. Among essentials, *Shooting Times* recommended:

> . . . thick boots with low, broad heels, stiff leather round back and sides of uppers, and plenty of hob-nails in soles and heels. Nails should be of wrought iron, for they take a better grip than steel ones. On getting home, put your boots onto wooden boot trees, lace them up and oil them wet (Neatsfoot oil is good stuff). Place the trees on the kitchen mantelshelf, where the boots will dry slowly and not get too hot.

For headgear, 'nothing beats a soft felt hat. It turns rain and shades you from the sun. Cloth caps get soaked and soon become shapeless.' And as for a mackintosh,

> Waterproofs merely make you hot and retain perspiration, so that you are as wet inside as out. Rain never killed anyone yet, and if you change when you get home you will be no worse for your outing. Colds are caught by sleeping or sitting in stuffy and ill-ventilated rooms, not out in the fresh air. Wear a flannel shirt and a good tweed suit, and you will take no harm.

But in these more practical days there was much new concession to comfort. In really hot weather, when shooting over dogs or walking-up, 'a tie with even a soft collar is irksome. To feel really free dispense with both and wear a silk handkerchief loosely round your neck, cowboy style.'

In 1928 the King left for the north on 15 August, when the Queen began a series of visits in the south. But he did not make his customary visit to Bolton Abbey as the prospects in Yorkshire were not good, owing to disease. For him grouse-shooting was obviously a real joy and came before many social considerations. He knew where the action was and would be at Balmoral towards the end of August.

There was little chance of the King grouse-shooting in Ireland, though he and the Queen went there after the Coronation. 'Hibernicus' of *Shooting Times* reported:

Some of us can remember very good grouse-shooting in the west and south of Ireland, and that over moors where the poacher has long ago wiped out the last grouse. I am afraid that the projected improvements in the Game Laws are very much like closing the stable door and locking it with great care about 10 years after the steed has been stolen.

The illicit disposal of dead grouse had, in Ireland, become a fine art.

The King apart, greatly increasing costs were affecting most sportsmen, and even the 'well-to-do' were having to cut down on staff. *Shooting Times* noted that:

'The Twelfth of August' by George Stratton-Ferrier (Courtesy of the Tryon Gallery)

Since the advent of the motor a sort of combination servant has arisen, a man who acts as chauffeur, valet, and loader, and since he has arrived very few gamekeepers are seen loading for their employers. This is to be regretted, for the occasional visits a keeper paid to other shoots had great educational value.

In fact, the magazine generally felt rather sorry for the moorland keeper in 1928:

If there is one man who thoroughly welcomes the Twelfth it is the moorland keeper, especially when he feels assured of showing good sport. His existence is rather a lonely one, particularly on remote moors, and were it not for the fact that he has plenty to do life might be extremely dull. It is a sad day for him when the last shooting party leaves. He welcomes the galaxy of servants, chauffeurs, valets, loaders, which appears, and learns much from them of what the wide world is doing. There are also others, pretty ladies' maids, and housemaids, and if he is young and impressionable, they must surely appeal to him. Southrons they may be, but there are good-looking girls south of the Tweed, and they reach the grouse moor only during the shooting season.

But the grouse-keeper was a very resourceful man, and it was often largely his expertise which kept a moor in good shape when it acquired a new tenant who had not been brought up in the ways of the field. How could a died-in-the-wool city slicker be expected to know, for example, how to keep flies off shot grouse in hot weather. But our keeper did:

Dig a hole at every drive and fit sticks across it. Suspend the birds on these, place a bag over the hole which flies cannot penetrate, and lodge sods of turf over all. In this receptacle the birds will be cool and soon stiffen, and they should be collected and transferred to the home larder at evening when flies have ceased to trouble. The best larder of all at this time of year is a cave excavated in a hillside and made flyproof.

However, expert aid for all potential grouse-shooters was at hand. In 1933, following the growth of ecology, the Imperial Chemical Industries Game Research Association (later the Eley Game Advisory Station) was founded. Obviously it had a vested interest in that it wanted to increase cartridge sales, but under the direction of A. D. Middleton (a major force in the promotion of Ecology at Oxford), it set standards for a much wider approach to field ecology. This made possible formation of the Game Research Association in 1960, which in 1969 became the Game Conservancy, today's leading-light in the integration of game-shooting and conservation interests.

It was as well that such an unemotional, scientifically based body was launched then because an increasingly mobile public had already started to view our last wilderness areas with covetous eyes. In 1932 the ramblers' associations had undertaken a mass trespass over the Kinder Scout grouse moors in the Peak District. On 25 April, five hundred ramblers climbed the beauty spot till on a remote, high plateau their way was barred by a line of the Duke of Devonshire's keepers and watchers, accompanied by police. Not surprisingly, scuffles broke out, and five or six ramblers arrested ended up in gaol. As the intruders were apparently unarmed while some keepers carried sticks, there was a national outcry.

The argument seemed simple enough: a privileged few trying to preserve a wide expanse of open countryside for their own use and not allowing a rag-bag of people

Lunch party at Balmoral, 1933, with King George II of Greece (foreground, left), Major Levidis (background, left), Sir Derek Keppel (at end of table), and then left to right: Hon Alexander Hardinge, Neville Wigram, Sir Frederick Ponsonby, The Duke of York (Royal Archives, Windsor)

– mostly from nearby industrial towns – to disrupt traditional country life. But it was also seen as class warfare – proletariat against landowning aristocrat – and the emotions aroused have remained with us to this day. And although Kinder Scout is now open to the public, as indeed are many other such wild places, there is a more recent complication with the realisation that these last bastions of nature must be *guarded* against excessive disturbance by *all* men if wildlife is to flourish there (see Chapter 12).

Grouse Shooting, 1924.
The best cartridges to
use are——

——manufactured by

ELEY & KYNOCH

OBTAINABLE FROM ALL GUNMAKERS AND DEALERS

STEADY NERVES AND A CLEAR EYE

AFTER a day's shooting, even though the bag was small, you will feel it was worth while if you did yourself justice. Not scarcity, but missed birds and 'runners' spoil the day, and no man who is less than fit can be certain of killing cleanly.

A faint headache or the slightest trace of jumpiness is so fatal to good shooting that most people safeguard themselves by taking a dash of ENO's " Fruit Salt " before they start the day. ENO keeps the nerves braced and the eye clear.

ENO's "FRUIT SALT"
The World-Famed Effervescent Saline

Further disturbance was worrying *Shooting Times'* Yorkshire correspondent in 1935:

The effect of aeroplanes flying over the moors and the consequent scaring of grouse will be watched with interest this season, as a daily service has been inaugurated between an airport and a seaside resort. Our moor is in direct line of flight and there are about six planes over every day.

Other major worries that year included the Grouse Commission playing into the hands of heather-burners. Twenty years of excessive, often uncontrolled burning had encouraged the invasion of bracken, against which the war continues today, with expensive spraying by helicopter and on foot.

Misrepresentation in the press was also common, with the proverbial 'crack of the rifle on the Twelfth'. But British Guns were guilty of sniping too, as *Shooting Times'* Scottish Notes for 10 August, 1935 testify: 'Americans are arriving with their guns

ALL IN THE SAME BUTT.

Notabilities from the northern counties of England who are, or expected to be, on the moors this month for the grouse shooting.
Back Row, left to right: Lord Bingley, Lord Barnard, Sir Murrough Wilson, Lord Harewood, Sir P. Cunliffe-Lister, Lord Lonsdale, Color L. Ropner, M.P., Mr. Norman Field.
Front Row, left to right: Mr. Walter Runciman, M.P., Lord Gainsford, Lord Joicey, Lord Rochdale, Lord Allendale, Lord Furness, Lo Bolton, Major T. L. Dugdale, M.P.

His first 'Twelfth' (1935)

and rifles at the lodges, and one at least has a rifle which is carried in a "cowboy" holster. I wonder how going up to red deer on a broncho would work.' But with storm clouds gathering over Europe again, it would not be long before such sporting bigots would welcome a Yankee invasion with open arms.

In August 1939 the sporting journals were full of despondency. On 5 August *The Field* reported:

This year will be one of the worst in the history of grouse-shooting. Apart from the fact that I hear Ichabods from Yorkshire and lamentations from Angus, the international situation has made it the worst letting year in history. The word Danzig has been even more damping than strongylosis. One of the most famous letting agents in the country assured me that he had only let one moor without a war clause.

Memory turned to World War I and consideration of how that conflict had irreversibly upset the sporting apple-cart:

Vast areas changed hands in 1919, notably the sale of a very big acreage by the Duke of Sutherland. Prices remained high till 1929, and today they are still above the pre-war level. The syndicate came to stay. Far more syndicate parties are to be found in Scottish lodges today than were ever found in the past, though the earliest reference to a grouse syndicate goes back to 1838.

Nonetheless, with stiff upper lip, *The Field* would urge readers to make the best of 'a rum do', calling on the most conservative of pens to rally the ranks. Lord Dorchester, for example, said it was 'impossible to contemplate the coming 12th with our usual joyful anticipation; indeed, by the time these lines are printed the cyclone may have burst, but there is still hope that the clouds may lift without discharging their lightnings.'

Dorchester lived partly in a dream world, where the main consideration was how easily the next shoot could be completed:

If you have but a single visit in view or are pressed for time, it probably simplifies matters to go by train, but if you are the lucky possessor of several invitations then a car is a great convenience, almost a necessity, indeed. Without a car you are tied to the railways, and probably to railway hotels between visits; with a car you not only avoid the bugbear of cross-country train journeys which are notoriously tiresome in Scotland, but can also fill in your time by touring the country at your leisure, and often are able to accept one or two extra invitations which would otherwise be inaccessible to you.

Sorting the grouse at Gunnerside. Young birds fetch higher prices from gamedealers

Overleaf: Walking up to the first drive at Gunnerside. Fitness is essential on the grouse moor

1935: grouse-shooters leaving King's Cross station for Scotland

His Grace The Duke of Roxburghe, on his Byrecleugh shoot, where let days are available

War or no war looming, the King was not going to miss out either: he was at Balmoral for the Twelfth, and as there had been no disease that year he found a good stock of birds. But for sheer nostalgia, *The Field*'s staff outshone their contributors in that August of impending doom. In their leader headed 'Going North' they discussed the traditional scenes at King's Cross, Euston and St Pancras. These places retained much of the atmosphere, but:

What is chiefly missed are the pointers and setters, though of course many dogs go by car. There is something about a brace of pointers, a gun case and a bag of cartridges that is redolent of an era which at times seems to be slipping away into the limbo of the past. They represent the more leisured and contented existence of our forebears, who had time to drink in each shooting scene and extract therefrom the acme of all it offered.

Shooting insurance with Norwich Union (1935)

AUGUST 12TH!

3-Garment Shooting Kit
BURBERRY SUIT
with Burberry Pivot Sleeves

Pivot Sleeves allow such absolute freedom for arm-swing and shoulder-play, that men who shoot quickly notice a marked improvement in their skill when wearing a Burberry Shooting Suit;

and

THE BURBERRY

—the Weatherproof Overcoat that satisfies the sportsman's every need. Keeps him dry when it rains, warm when it is chilly, comfortable under every conceivable change of weather or temperature.

The man who includes these two items in his kit for the moors makes fewer misses, cleaner "kills" and shoots at perfect ease, completely protected whether it rains, blows or swelters.

BURBERRY GAMEFEATHER SUITS

For shooting suits, the best possible camouflage is Burberry Gamefeather Tweeds, which are woven in the colours and on the principles of the plumage of gamebirds. These beautiful suitings are now available in fine Saxonies as well as Scotch Cheviots. There are many model suits to choose from, each different in design, yet all planned to adjust weight, free the arms and shoulders, and add to the pleasure of shooting by ease, balance and elimination of restriction.

THE BURBERRY

Weightless—wind-proof, rain-proof, drizzle-proof—naturally ventilating—The Burberry provides a delightful Overcoat and perfect Weatherproof.

Designed on easy-fitting lines from thin and flexible materials, it makes no difference to the "set" of the gun, and is the one coat in which the "shot" can maintain top form comfortably protected against wet, wind and cold.

Patterns and full particulars sent on mention of "The Field."

BURBERRYS LTD. HAYMARKET LONDON, S.W.1

The Car of a Hundred-and-One Utilities
Is The New FORD V-8
UTILITY CAR,

Completely equipped, as illustrated, £260, with the standard seating-accommodation for eight (including driver)

For station or staff transport, shooting, fishing, golfing, and general sporting service, comfortably roomy, smart and trim in appearance, although an essentially utilitarian model.

The mere possession of this latest Ford V-8 will reveal a surprising number of jobs which it will perform to admiration.

In design and construction its bodywork maintains Ford V-8 standards; and its finish and trimming are of a type to withstand the carrying of luggage, parcels, supplies, stores or sporting impedimenta. And of course the performance is Ford V-8 performance, an exemplary combination of efficiency and economy — particularly fuel-economy, because the V-8 engine does the maximum amount of its work, anywhere, on top gear. Literature on Request: All Prices at Works: Dealers Everywhere.

FORD MOTOR COMPANY LIMITED, WORKS: DAGENHAM, ESSEX. LONDON SHOWROOMS: 88 REGENT STREET, W.1

Shooting brake advertisement (1937)

However, all was not lost: the 'peace and charm of the eternal hills' were still there and so 'with a light heart and a composed mind we may set our course towards those Elysian fields and wake to the purple moors . . .' Purple prose indeed.

In 1940 the grouse-shooting season was advanced by Order in Council to 5 August, and, more importantly, the law prohibiting the killing of game on Sundays in England and Wales was suspended. *Shooting Times* reported: 'Birds are likely to be plentiful, while sportsmen and cartridges will be fewer and gamekeepers will shoot over many grouse-moors, for it is essential to keep the stock within reasonable bounds in order to prevent an outbreak of disease.' However, the magazine regretted that insufficient notice of the change had been given and feared that 'more harm than good may accrue. In the first place, the arrangements of those who shoot on the opening date have been upset.' The editor suggested that the season be extended to 7 January as 'there is no doubt that quite a large number of shooting men would take the opportunity ot spending a period round Christmas on the moors.' As it was, it was most unfortunate that there would be insufficient Guns to deal with a large head of grouse arising from little shooting in the preceding year and an excellent breeding season. Another thing they had not bargained on that season was large areas of moor being set alight by enemy bombs, as happened on 31 August near Helmsley, Yorkshire, small parties of grouse being seen at night near the Malton road.

Shooting Times was equally vociferous in its criticism of another temporary measure:

A proposal that Home Guard officers and men should do some grouse-shooting this season was made in a Scottish newspaper, but the H.G. are working men, and few of them can afford to take other than the legally allowable holidays. Nor could the rank and file of the Home Guard afford to buy cartridges, and the waste of gratis ammunition would be enormous.

Ford's utility car on the grouse moor (1935)

Overall, there was a lot of unrest regarding temporary wartime shooting seasons, as explained by *The Field* in 1944:

The decision of Whitehall that the date for the opening of grouse-shooting shall not be again advanced this year will have been welcomed as much by all serious shooting men as it will by many others who will regard it as a first promising sign that completely deaf ears may in future be no longer turned upon the voice of sound reason and hard, practical exprience. For except in the just-possible case of soldiers on leave who were due to return to duty before the traditional

Pettits of Reedham gamedealers' advertisement (1940s)

The Twelfth

Over the Moor   Drawing by Wilfred S. Pettitt

Grouse on the moor.
Mallard over broadland.
Geese by the sandhill.
Snipe midst the bracken.
Woodcock dodging swiftly
    among the tree trunks.
The Game is on.

There is no finer market in the country than

PETTITTS of REEDHAM Ltd.
NORWICH   NORFOLK

*We pay full control price and carriage for Game
and a generous fixed price for classified Wildfowl*

SCOTLAND!

Night trains for "The Twelfth"

A cavalcade of comfortable sleeping car trains speed through the night to Scotland for The Glorious Twelfth and across the border in the early morning the rested traveller is presented with a marvellous vista of colourful Scottish moorland. Travel by night to Scotland from King's Cross, Euston or St. Pancras. It is a pleasant restful interlude between the glamour of Mayfair and the scent of the heather-clad hills. A list of these comfortably equipped night trains with first and third-class sleeping accommodation is given below and on the trains leaving London before 8.0 p.m. you may dine in comfort. The times of day trains will be supplied on request at any L·N·E·R or L M S station, office or agency.

FROM KING'S CROSS (L·N·E·R)

WEEKDAYS AND SUNDAYS

P.M.
*7.25R "The Highlandman" — Edinburgh, Fort William (Breakfast car attached *en route*), Perth, Inverness.
*7.40R "The Aberdonian" —Edinburgh, Dundee, Aberdeen, Elgin, Lossiemouth.
†10.25 "The Night Scotsman" —Glasgow, Dundee, Aberdeen, Perth.
†10.35 Edinburgh. (North Berwick

first class only and on Friday nights only.)
A.M.
¶1.5 After-Theatre Sleeping and Breakfast Car Train, Edinburgh, connection to Glasgow, Dundee, Aberdeen, Perth, Inverness.
* Nightly (except Saturdays). † Nightly. ¶Daily (except Sunday mornings). R Restaurant Car King's Cross to York.

FROM EUSTON (L M S)

P.M.   WEEKDAYS
7.20AB "The Royal Highlander"—Perth, Boat of Garten, Inverness, Aberdeen.
7.25AB Oban.
7.40AB Stirling, Gleneagles.
8.0A Dumfries, Stranraer Harbour, Turnberry, Ayr.
9.15 Glasgow (Cent.) (Fridays only).
9.25 Glasgow (Fridays excepted). (On Saturdays, Third Class Sleeping Accommodation only).
10.50 Edinburgh.
10.50F Stirling, Gleneagles, Perth, Oban, Dundee, Aberdeen, Inverness.
10.55D Stirling, Gleneagles, Perth, Oban, Dundee, Aberdeen, Inverness.
11.45 "Night Scot"—Glasgow.

A.M.
12.20DE Dumfries, Kilmarnock, Ayr, Turnberry, Glasgow (St. Enoch).

P.M.   SUNDAYS
7.20B "The Royal Highlander"—Perth, Boat of Garten, Inverness.

7.30B Stirling, Oban, Gleneagles, Perth, Dundee, Aberdeen,

8.30 Dumfries, Stranraer Harbour, Ayr, Turnberry.

9.30 Glasgow (Cent.).

10.50 Edinburgh, Stirling, Gleneagles, Perth, Dundee, Aberdeen, Inverness, Oban.

11.45 "Night Scot"—Glasgow.

NOTES : A *Saturdays excepted.* B *Restaurant Car.* D *Saturday nights and Sunday mornings excepted.* E *Sleeping Cars to Kilmarnock.* F *Saturday nights only.*

FROM ST. PANCRAS (L M S)

P.M.   WEEKDAYS
9.15 Edinburgh, (Waverley), Dundee, Perth, Inverness, Aberdeen.
9.30 Dumfries, Kilmarnock, Ayr, Turnberry (no arrival Sun.) Glasgow (St. Enoch)

P.M.   SUNDAYS
9.15 Edinburgh (Waverley), Dundee, Perth, Inverness, Aberdeen.
9.33 Dumfries, Kilmarnock, Ayr. Turnberry, Glasgow, (St. Enoch).

CHEAP MONTHLY RETURN TICKETS — With a cheap Monthly Return Ticket you have the choice of East Coast, West Coast or Midland routes, in either direction, with break of journey at any station.
MOTOR CARS — Motor Cars accompanied by one first-class or two third-class adult passengers are conveyed by Rail to include outward and homeward journeys at reduced rates.

IT'S QUICKER BY RAIL!

LONDON & NORTH EASTERN RLY. ● LONDON MIDLAND & SCOTTISH RLY.

opening date, it has been difficult to discern what deserving persons or legitimate interests have been served by these official rulings which have characterised the war-time seasons. It is, indeed, very doubtful whether anyone has reaped any real recreational advantage from such arbitrary and ill-considered interference.

As the war ended, grouse-shooting was at a very low ebb – the 1945 season was one of the worst on record. Few moors were let, young birds were scarce almost everywhere, gillies and 'drivers' (beaters) were practically unobtainable, and the demand for cartridges was very small. However, the undaunted *Shooting Times* wrote of a 'spirit of optimism' and hoped that 'each succeeding season may show an improvement in the stock of birds, particularly as keepers will shortly be available to wage war against vermin that has increased during the war years.'

Grouse were still shot over dogs on some Scottish moors but 'driving is nowadays the almost universal practice. Grand as it is to watch pointers or setters quartering, shooting over dogs is a less social form of sport than driving, which appeals to a host who wishes to entertain a house party.' In addition, there was 'the diverse way in which birds come to the butts. They appear at all angles, elevation, and pace, depending on the wind, the character of the ground, and the situation of your battery.'

There were new problems on the horizon – overhead wires, for example. *Shooting Times'* grouse expert Dugald Macintyre wrote: 'Electric wires, in combination with telephone and telegraph ones, stretched across our mountain-sides, make it impossible for grouse to thrive. Not so long ago I saw seven grouse killed when one pack impacted on a mass of telephone and electric wires.'

World War II might have been over, but there were innumerable little battles to fight in trying to regain a healthy grouseland.

7

A Bad Press

From the fifties to the eighties, grouse-shooters joined other fieldsportsmen in a constant struggle against inaccurate media representation and 'antis'

In the fifties there was a noticeable increase in the number of ladies visiting moors to take part in the sport rather than act only as lunch companions, as generally had been the position in the past. However, the percentage of female Guns has not changed much since then. It had been the great increase in the number of motor cars which had encouraged ladies to share in the northern season. Once they arrived, their more gracious influence turned buildings that had previously been little better than sporting doss-houses into comfortable homes. This change (combined with increasingly heavy taxation of our landed proprietors) in turn led to the letting of grouse-moors to foreigners, because those wealthy incomers appreciated, and demanded, the domestic luxury which many of our lairds could no longer afford to maintain, except in their permanent residences. Thus, by the mid-fifties the letting of a moor depended as much on the condition of the lodge as on the annual bag.

Another major change was the large increase in servicemen now visiting the moors. Mostly young Army officers, they had sampled the glorious grouse during the war years, when few other Guns were available, and had become addicted to the sport. Unfortunately, many of them, as well as a large contingent of other newcomers, had not been brought up in the ways of traditional country pursuits and needed careful supervision in matters of safety and etiquette as well as education in natural history. But then, this is a problem which has been with us ever since, with all game-shooting growing in popularity every year.

In 1957 Harold Macmillan told voters that they had 'never had it so good', and there is no doubt that the extra cash and leisure time generally available from then on has provided the sport with a real boost.

Two years later the Nature Conservancy inaugurated its Unit of Grouse and Moorland Ecology, at Aberdeen University. And while the boffins began their seemingly unending search for answers to age-old mysteries such as periodic decline of grouse populations, the quality of sport could scarcely be improved. Research would be most important in ensuring continuity of a sport increasingly seen as a pillar of the rural economy and the key to upland conservation.

On the social scene, the Macmillan years saw increasing interest in the annual 'grouse race', when fashionable hotels, clubs and restaurants vie with each other to become the first with that season's grouse on the menu. And the *bon viveurs* demonstrated glorious one-upmanship in their desire to sample the first succulent mouthful. Elaborate arrangements were made for express delivery – not only in this country, but also in America and other places abroad – constituting a romance of

their own. This really was something for the popular press to get its well-filled teeth into, but even they could not envisage how the race would develop in later years, with helicopters standing by to take the first grouse to the breakfast tables of leading hotels.

In 1965 *Shooting Times'* contributor J. K. Stanford (author of the popular little book *The Twelfth*) asked: 'Who first gave that date the faintly derisive adjective 'glorious'? He added: 'I do not think it was a sporting man.' Perhaps for those days he was not being too pedantic, but today the word glorious, in this context, is generally accepted

Flying grouse tend to hug the contours of the land. Painting by Archibald Thorburn (Courtesy of the Tryon Gallery)

by all and harbours few overtones. The sport *is* glorious, the heather moor *is* glorious, and the grouse *is* glorious in the eyes of the hunter.

More telling was Stanford's condemnation of increasing inaccurate reportage concerning the Twelfth. He pointed to press jargon such as 'slaughter of the innocents, when the gentlemen from the south arrive for a week's sport, hoping to outdo one another in the number of little corpses in their bags.' And, of course, he went on to defend the pursuit. Unfortunately, however, he had the same problem which sporting scribes have to this day, in that he had plenty of opportunity to preach to the converted, but few chances to present supportive, scientific facts to the general public.

In another article, Stanford asked:

What exactly is the typical grouse-moor image, of which we hear so much nowadays, and which is said to be as non-vote-catching as halitosis or a squint? I know many politicians, of all shades of opinion, who would look, and doubtless feel, as incongruous and unhappy on a moor as a flamingo or a spoonbill.

He rightly pointed to sheer ignorance of basic facts as the main problem.

Not surprisingly, in this new era of public criticism, many shoots were fearful of any publicity and from then on the shooting magazines found it increasingly difficult to get and publish comprehensive reports including actual names of people and places. Many proprietors decided that keeping a low profile would be best to counter the rising 'anti' element. And only now, as we enter the make-or-break nineties, are hitherto secretive shoot proprietors daring to come out of the closet because they have a mass of new scientific information on their side.

Ironically, when it came to assessing the 1965 season overall, the editor of *Shooting Times* singled out for special criticism the *Daily Mail*, the flagship publication of Associated Newspapers, the company which now also owns *Shooting Times*. Apparently, a heading in the *Daily Mail* issue of 16 August repeated the word bang seventeen times, followed by the caption 'And ONE little grouse bites the dust'. *Shooting Times* retorted:

Never mind why it was a *little* grouse: the important point is the ratio of kills-cartridges. But this article, unlike most, did not stop at the actual shooting season, for it told us what happens after the Guns have returned from their sport on the moors. 'They go back to their offices to sort out the business deals they've discussed on the moors.' (There's enormous pride among the gamekeepers when they hear that, say, a million pound deal was clinched on *their* moor. They feel they've engineered it personally. So a good employer tells his gamekeeper. Discreet men, these gamekeepers, but they know a good many trade secrets by the end of the season.)

One aspect that did need improving in the sixties was the general attitude to shooting safety, but it was an uphill struggle against 'the old school', who resented any change. They did not appreciate that with so many more people coming into field-sports, from all walks of life, behaviour had to be exemplary.

In August 1965, David Imrie, a highly respected *Shooting Times*' contributor, wrote:

If the stopping place should happen to be beside a dry-stone wall, the empty

Durward clothes for the moor (1934)

guns are more often than not propped against it, but experienced shooting men pay strict attention that no insecure stones are overhanging their weapons. And they also make certain that it cannot fall on chunks of rock, if a dog should knock it over accidentally.

Imrie seemed concerned only for the gun, but today we would frown on anyone who puts a gun down closed, let alone stand it up, as a closed gun is rightly seen as potentially loaded and therefore dangerous. Today it is also customary to open your gun while in company, so that your companions can see it is not loaded, but some older Shots still find it hard to break the habits of half a century.

Imrie's main topic was lunch on the moor. He described how, at some of the more fashionable establishments, it was still customary for the butler to be present, 'although he generally removes himself after the preliminaries, so that the shooters are free to talk.' But being a keeper, he was specially interested in the servants' food: 'It is still common for keepers and loaders to have their lunch sent out from the lodge, though beaters fetch their own nourishment.' For the more important assistants, these lunches were 'generally sandwiches plus cake, cheese and beer or lemonade'. In his experience, such lunches were 'first class, both in quality and quantity'. But he could remember grumbles from retainers who wanted variety. 'To my surprise, the owner ordered several kinds of meat to accompany a box of buttered bread, so that each man could make up sandwiches to his own taste.' The cheese which he had seen most often on the moor was Wensleydale,

> . . . lovely stuff, made in the local farmhouse. Ordinary persons would have eaten this with the buttered bread, but the keepers, who were Yorkshiremen, invariably ate it with cake. One fellow always sat with a hunk of cheese in one hand and *two* slabs of cake in the other, from which he took enormous bites alternately.

Keepers, beaters and Guns all appreciated the huge improvements which had been made in shoot transport. In the old days there were few cars or lorries to take Guns and beaters to the moor so long-distance travelling on the day of a shoot was out of

A covey approaches; great concentration is essential

FOR THE MOORS
Gamefeather–Camouflage

For shooting suits, the best possible camouflage is Game-feather Tweeds which are woven in the colours and on the principles of the plumage of gamebirds. These beautiful suitings are now available in fine Saxonies as well as Scotch Cheviots.

Burberry suits for shooting — there are many designs — provide perfect freedom. Pivot sleeves, a Burberry invention, release arms and shoulders from all sense of restraint.

Burberrys advertisement (1938)

BURBERRYS LTD. HAYMARKET LONDON, S.W.1

the question. Early vehicles were unsuitable for cross-country work and there were few reasonable roads across the moors. Thus the lessee of a moor and his party generally made their headquarters close by, at the shooting box (lodge). From there journeys had to be made on foot, only a few Guns choosing to move from drive to drive by pony. Other ponies were fitted with panniers, to carry the spare cartridges and the grouse which were bagged.

By the sixties, shoot transport had been revolutionised. Land-Rovers had become universal, capable of tackling most terrain, and for the more difficult areas there were Snowcats. Such increasing comforts attracted more and more people to the sport and made the keeper's life far easier. But it also meant that fewer keepers were needed. And with such economies and greater income, shoot proprietors could begin the expensive programme of road-making across the moors, a worthwhile investment for the future.

Nowadays, transport poses few problems and if any ponies remain they are creatures of nostalgia, not that this is a bad thing in an age of rush and tear. Not everyone wants to Concorde over the Atlantic from the States, hop aboard a chopper for grouseland and dash about in a Range Rover like something without legs. Slower transport brings a slowing down of mental processes and inevitably means greater satisfaction. That said, swift and reliable transport is most important for those who are unfit or constantly live both business and private lives in the fast lane, so that time is always at a premium.

In the seventies improved communications, ease of international travel, and further commercialisation of shooting brought many more foreigners to grouseland as well as to the pheasant coverts. Americans continued to be associated with the best let days, but gradually German, Dutch, French, Belgian and Italian shooters became commonplace on moderately expensive moors. Unfortunately, this difficult sport was a revelation to many of them, they often lost their heads and behaved dangerously. The French and Italians, in particular, have long been associated with swinging dangerously through the line. Not only that, some of them find other quarry – both protected and unprotected – irresistible. Back at home skylarks have always been regarded as a delicacy, and getting Italians to ignore the many hares which run between the butts is asking a lot. Today some moors have solved the problem – they ask Continentals back for special January hare shoots, at a very considerable premium of course!

Both proprietors and sporting agents soon realised that large bonuses were to be earned in providing complete shooting-holiday packages, including accommodation. But increasing commercialisation means greater reliance on guaranteed bags, both to keep the roof on the crumbling pile and avoid dissatisfied customers, who might easily defect to greener moors over the hill. Thus the seventies saw ever-greater interest in the season's prospects. Experts were called upon to predict the effects of weather, breeding success, disease and so on, for what had become big business.

Of course, we get exceptional years in which everything looks rosy nationwide, but in the main our weather brings considerable regional variation, and with patchy prospects the forecaster has to stick his neck out. In a way, it is sad that the shooting

Taking a shot behind. Gloves and ear muffs are sensible precautions in concentrated driven shooting

community must take such an interest in co-ordination and organisation because in the end it is partly the unpredictability of grouse-shooting, and the inevitable varying fortunes of a truly wild quarry species which make the grouse a king and the reared, released pheasant only a pretender to the throne. And with organisers under increasing pressure to fulfil obligations, it is not surprising that some old keepers look back on more relaxed, all-guest private days with misty eyes.

During the seventies and eighties grouse research really got underway, chiefly prompted by financial interests. Of various projects, perhaps the most important was the North of England Grouse Research Project, 1977–85, culminating in the important technical report 'Red Grouse – The Biology and Management of a Wild Gamebird', written by Peter Hudson and published by the Game Conservancy Trust in 1986. It was sixty-seven years since Lord Lovat's report and new technology had made monitoring the bird much easier. Significant decreases in grouse density in many areas attracted the support of moor-owners who had come to rely on grouse for much of their income. The object was to identify major factors influencing grouse populations and to propose methods to increase grouse production, to enable moors to maintain viable shooting stocks and avoid selling out to alternative land uses.

Further pressures arose when farmers, foresters, conservationists and ramblers took increasing interest in remaining heather moorland – about 400,000ha (1 million acres) in England and Wales and about twice this in Scotland, a surprisingly large acreage considering so much had already been lost. Fortunately, ecologists soon came to realise that without grouse-shooting interests a wide range of species would be endangered. Farmers, too, were made more aware of grouse as an *additional* source of income. The key factor was getting heather widely accepted as a valuable *crop*.

Some areas, such as the west and central Highlands, were carrying too many deer and sheep for the good of grouse, but with certain aspects of agriculture in decline it was hoped that the position would soon improve. A reduction in the number of keepers overall was also a problem in that predators had been allowed to proliferate. Those few moors fortunate to have enough men on the hill have been fighting a losing battle in that as soon as they remove foxes more come in from adjoining unkeepered ground or new forestry. In addition, predatory birds have proliferated, but some of these are rightly now protected.

Fortunately, towards the end of the eighties there was an upswing in grouse numbers after a protracted decline in some regions, so the decade ended on a high note, with good driven days once again a viable proposition. But costs were rising dramatically and it was no surprise that there was renewed interest in the cheaper, old-style walked-up shooting, especially with the wider, popular curiosity in the ways of yesteryear. Even people with the cash to buy any sport on offer became interested in rougher, more energetic forms of shooting, as part of a general movement to achieve that clichéd 'oneness with nature', to get 'closer to the land'. They welcomed the opportunity for what they saw as true hunting, outwitting the quarry on its own ground, with the actual killing playing a relatively minor role.

This, in turn, led to greater interest in the dual-purpose gundog breeds which point and retrieve, such as the German shorthaired pointer. Such breeds remove the necessity and expense of keeping specialist pointing breeds – dogs which have to be kept all year for only a few weeks' work.

Hunters of grouse have also been subject to pressures affecting all shooters. Although the eighties undoubtedly saw a weakening of the anti-bloodsports movement, as fieldsportsmen enlisted the aid of scientific argument and got their public relations act together, gun ownership itself came under public scrutiny. Some police forces became increasingly obstructive in their interpretation of the Firearms Act and, often quite unjustifiably, sought to restrict legal gun ownership, penalising sportsmen generally for the outrageous acts of a criminal minority, such as Michael Ryan at Hungerford.

In addition, game-shooters have been subject to increasing self-examination, as enthusiasts generally have at last realised that certain perfectly legal, but undesirable shooting practices would jeopardise future sport. Thus, in 1989, the shooting organisations had no alternative but to draft a code of practice, condemning activities such as the release of birds after the start of the shooting season. It was an affront to the dignity of the mass of sportsmen schooled in traditional ways, but an important expediency in countering the worst aspects of commercialisation and sheer pressure of numbers. Fortunately, the grouse-shooter has been spared this inquisition because his quarry is not reared and released and is almost always a wild and worthy mark. However, increasing strictures on pheasant-shooting may well have repercussions on the moor as frustrated covert-bashers defect to the heather.

That said, grouse-shooting has survived remarkably well during two centuries of great social and environmental change. In the beginning it was chiefly the pursuit of those who inherited wealth and privilege – the so-called leisured classes – and a sprinkling of 'high-achievers', to use current jargon. But now it is the pastime of everyman and as long as we can control this growth of interest with proper respect for sportsmanship and the natural world grouse-shooting will have a healthy future.

Counting the bag on the Biddulphs' Lammermuirs shoot

8

The Keeper's Story

In the old days keepers had to be tough to face autocratic bosses as well as harsh moorland weather. Willie Veitch was such a man

The present Duke of Westminster, a keen grouse-shooter and owner of the famous Abbeystead Moor, once told me that a good grouse-keeper should look like a grouse. Mere rhetoric, of course, but there is no denying that a good grouse-keeper must *think* like a grouse. One of the most successful was Willie Veitch, who put in forty-four years for the Duke of Roxburghe and other distinguished moor-owners.

Willie is a great character of the true old school who has worked with pheasant, partridge, salmon and deer, but is mostly known for his work with grouse. Born in Duns, Berwickshire, on 22 February, 1922, he now lives in peaceful rural retirement with his wife Jean, his sharp memory recalling life on the hill. Only sudden ill-health forced him to take it easy and you can sense his frustration as he looks out over the Borders countryside which he has done so much to preserve.

As with other great keepers, much of Willie's strength of character came from having to cope with equally forceful masters – autocrats who organised sport purely for themselves and their friends. They had no truck with selling shooting, and thus no need to kowtow to those who are generally ingratiatingly called 'paying guests' rather than customers. They could say and do what they wished and had no hesitation in condemning ungentlemanly and unsporting behaviour, banishing forever even the most noble for a breech of etiquette.

Willie started helping a local keeper while he was still at school.

Keepering was very much a closed shop then – you had to have relatives known in the job to get accepted. Anyway, I began with butt building and cutting bracken with a whankey, a long pole with a hook. I was just eleven then, and on my holidays.

There were far less sheep then and thus less damage to the butts, so that less protective fencing was needed. I've moved four lines of butts in my time, but the principal drives are the same, though partly extended. The late duke wouldn't sanction turf butts without trying experimental ones first, but the grouse would shy off from these temporary stand-up butts and then sometimes you had to go by instinct in planning a line.

On leaving school at fourteen, Willie was persuaded to ignore a kennel boy vacancy and instead went into a garage to 'learn a trade'. He did this up to the outbreak of war, but continued to visit Rawburn, then owned by the Duke of Roxburghe, to help keeper Andrew Riddel. In 1940 he joined the Navy as a volunteer, and on returning

The Duke of Westminster and his loader on his famous Abbeystead Moor. Such stone butts blend well with the landscape

in 1946 went to work on grouse and deer, as underkeeper for Lord Galloway at Glen Trool, Wigtownshire.

The Forestry Commission was only just getting into its stride and they had great gangs of men instead of tractors. Unfortunately they didn't fence in the new trees and most were eaten by deer.

It was a hell of a place for foxes – very rocky, with cairns so deep you couldn't dig them. Sometimes we dropped gelignite down to stun them, but the river-watcher had his finger blown off. And it was hell to get terriers out. A real killer terrier (not many will kill a full-grown fox) would often stay with its kill and we had to rely on it coming out of its own accord.

Water traps were best for foxes. We used to set ginns around bait on an island, so that the foxes had to jump across and straight onto them. But that's all illegal now and Fenn traps would not hold them well enough in water. Next best was to bury a bait where foxes run regularly, leaving a little fur poking out the soil.

This was surrounded by ginns and highly productive.

The main emphasis then – and now – was on restricting the spread of vermin. There's a new name for it – oh yes, predators – mainly magpies, carrion crows, stoats and weasels as well as foxes.

In 1948 Willie replaced the retiring keeper at Byrecleugh, Andrew Riddel having contacted his father to ask if he would apply.

The late Duke of Roxburghe and his factor interviewed me at Floors Castle, and within a week I heard that I had been appointed – I was to report on . . . to the headkeeper. There was no question of you considering a job in those days.

I started on pheasants – we had just the one 'big week' then, all double guns, and there was damn little left when those fellows had finished. The bags were 250–350 a day and very few were reared. But numbers weren't important then. If it was a blustery day the Duke would stop at lunchtime and go pigeon-shooting – he didn't like to put pheasants on the neighbours' ground. This would not do! You see, wild birds were entirely different and would travel a long way, unlike the poor things you get now. And pigeon numbers were more consistent then – there was less packing and more variation.

The big week was held when the leaves had fallen and there was a maximum of just six Guns for the house party. As soon as they'd gone I was sent back to Byrecleugh for grouse work. Then when the snow came I tracked foxes, bolted them with terriers and shot them.

I stayed in the servants' hall at the old shooting lodge. I'm not sure what I earned, perhaps £3 a week at first, but in 1964 it was up to £39 for a month – look, I've still got one of the pay packets – plus £1 for your dog. Only one allowed: you had to pay for terriers.

It was in 1964 that my father gave me a half-sovereign, which I, in turn, have passed on. He said that as long as he had that coin he was never broke – very much a Scottish tradition.

Willie lived rent free and each year was given a new suit of clothes and wool for stockings, two lorry-loads of logs and 5 tons of coal:

. . . great stuff, bloody great chunks, not the rubbish you get now. And that coal had to serve for the cook when the Duke and his guests stayed at the lodge. Most of the time I lived on my own though, and I used to bake scones and everything.

The late Duke was no respector of persons – he called a spade a spade, dukes an' all. If thing's wern't going to plan he would even jump on top of a butt and wave and shout. He'd get in one hell of a state. Mind you, we never had an argument, only 'discussions', after which he'd tap his stick on the ground and go away chuckling to himself.

The old beater – fifty years on one estate

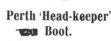

Advertisement for Norwell's range of boots for the keeper (1914)

He was a brilliant Shot. In fact, it's safe to say that when his valet, Chandler, loaded for him it was just like watching a machine – they weren't like two separate people. Charles Chandler went all over the place with him – even the Continent. He was a match for anyone – even people with two loaders and three guns.

It was always double guns then. The Duke had Stephen Grant sidelock sidelevers – full-choke in both barrels. I've never seen anybody else kill grouse so far out. A covey of grouse would come by him and the late Colonel Bill Stirling and between them they'd kill the lot.

At first Willie had to get about by push-bike as there were no roads on the estate. And as he was single-handed at Byrecleugh the keepers at Floors had to come up for a week or so to help him with the burning, especially as the acreage increased from

Over-and-unders are still uncommon on first-class grouse moors

Grouse netting (1915)

about 6,000 to over 12,000 in 1963. Burning has always been on a rotational strip system, but now they use a swipe on a tractor to cut a 6ft firebreak around each strip to be burnt. Willie continued:

> This gives so much more control, it has revolutionised burning. Mind you, the man on the beat must be the one to cut the strips as he is the only one who knows the ground well enough. The other men merely come along and burn back into the wind. You hardly get any of the massive conflagrations there used to be.
>
> Whatever I was doing, neither the old Duke nor the new one would ride roughshod over me. They asked my opinion and never talked down to me. A headkeeper really must have the courage of his convictions. Mind you, it's got me into trouble standing up and being counted, but if you're honest there's no way anybody can get behind you.

It was a lonely life out on the moor, especially without radio contact or fast transport, and the keeper really was dependent on the weather.

> You could get one hell of a grouse pack when the snow covered the heather, but then they would suddenly disperse. When a pack moved off to lower, easier ground the foxes would concentrate on them, thinning them out, so fewer came back.
>
> The winter of 1941 was a memorable one. I was away in the Navy, but father

told me the holly trees in Duns were black with grouse after the berries. Nowadays grouse seem to move much quicker with the snow than they used to. If there is no wind and the snow cover is total so that the birds can't feed, then they've got to go, especially if the surface thaws and then re-freezes to form a crust. We used to go out on the moor with a horse dragging a harrow – upside down so that it wouldn't catch the heather – to break up the snow for the birds. The grouse used to follow behind us just like crows behind a tractor and plough.

In 1954 Willie and his family had to leave Byrecleugh because his son could not get to school easily, so off he went to Lord Haddington's Mellerstain, as a pheasant beatkeeper. 'I didn't go nothing on that – rabbit catchin' was all they wanted, so I left after a year.' From there Willie moved to Candecraig, Strathdon, to spend nine

Hurdle advertisement of 1928

happy years as beatkeeper on grouse for Major A. F. (Dandy) Wallace, a well-known Shot. He left when he happened to go home for his mother's funeral, bumped into the Floors' headkeeper and was asked to go back to Byrecleugh. His time at Candecraig had been particularly enjoyable because he was also involved with salmon fishing and deerstalking, his favourite pastime.

The Duke used to have Millden in Angus as well as Byrecleugh and sometimes

. . . he shot solidly at the two for five or six days a week over six weeks, and played cards till two in the morning: I don't know how he did it. I used to go up to Millden to help out with the flanking or picking-up.

The attitude to the Twelfth was different in those days. Nine times out of ten there would be just a small party walking-up a few brace for the house and they would take lunch on the hill – usually family and friends, but not always the Duke. Later on, when they got down to the serious stuff the expense was fantastic – the old gentleman lived in a Victorian style we just can't imagine. The guests paid nothing, apart from tips – about a pound or thirty bob each back in the forties, but £15–20 nowadays.

We've had some real characters on the moor. I've seen some real palavers after lunchtime – ladies too. Lord . . . once threw one of the ladies into the pool by the lunch hut – he's never been back. And you wouldn't believe what went on in butts, especially when the drink was flowing.

Today most grouse-keepers look forward to their own shooting day at the end of the season, just as pheasant-keepers do. However, Willie

. . . wouldn't let them have it for years. Now all the keepers are quite good Shots, but many of them practise on clay-pigeons. I never had the money. I was there to produce grouse for *gentlemen* to shoot, not keepers.

Do you know, I've never taken a holiday since the war, and when I became ill this season I just couldn't accept it. I used to work all day long humping great big stones around, and I was devastated when, for the first time, I couldn't walk to the hill.

Not surprisingly, Willie does not enjoy eating grouse: 'I wouldn't go overboard for them; in fact I usually give them away. But venison, that's something else, especially the saddle suitably seasoned – no garlic though – and made into steaks with the bone taken out.'

Grouse-keepers certainly need 'stoking up' for the hill. 'We never needed a topcoat,' Willie told me, 'what with the tweed the way it was – not like the rubbish you get now. Mind you, if you had a steepin' (soaking) you'd need a small pony to carry it.'

Willie also has very strong views when it comes to predator control and vigorously defends the keeper's record.

Right: *The flanker must know exactly when to wave his flag to turn grouse*

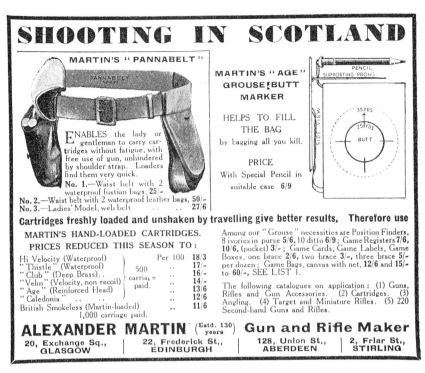

SHOOTING IN SCOTLAND

MARTIN'S "PANNABELT"

ENABLES the lady or gentleman to carry cartridges without fatigue, with free use of gun, unhindered by shoulder strap. Loaders find them very quick.

No. 1.—Waist belt with 2 waterproof fustian bags, **25/-**
No. 2.—Waist belt with 2 waterproof leather bags, **50/-**
No. 3.—Ladies' Model, web belt   .. **27/6**

MARTIN'S "AGE" GROUSE BUTT MARKER

HELPS TO FILL THE BAG
by bagging all you kill.

PRICE
With Special Pencil in suitable case **6/9**

Cartridges freshly loaded and unshaken by travelling give better results.   Therefore use

MARTIN'S HAND-LOADED CARTRIDGES.
PRICES REDUCED THIS SEASON TO:

Hi Velocity (Waterproof)	Per 100	**18/3**
"Thistle" (Waterproof)	500	**17/-**
"Club" (Deep Brass)..	carriage	**16/-**
"Velm" (Velocity, non-recoil)	paid.	**14/-**
"Age" (Reinforced Head)		**13/6**
"Caledonia" ..		**12/6**
British Smokeless (Martin-loaded)		**11/6**
1,000 carriage paid.		

Among our "Grouse" necessities are Position Finders, 8 ivories in purse **5/6**, 10 ditto **6/9**; Game Registers **7/6**, **10/6**, (pocket) **3/-** ; Game Cards, Game Labels, Game Boxes, one brace **2/6**, two brace **3/-**, three brace **5/-** per dozen; Game Bags, canvas with net, **12/6** and **15/-** to **60/-**, SEE LIST I.

The following catalogues on application : (1) Guns, Rifles and Gun Accessories. (2) Cartridges. (3) Angling. (4) Target and Miniature Rifles. (5) 220 Second-hand Guns and Rifles.

ALEXANDER MARTIN (Estd. 130 years) Gun and Rifle Maker

| 20, Exchange Sq., GLASGOW | 22, Frederick St., EDINBURGH | 128, Union St., ABERDEEN | 2, Friar St., STIRLING |

Martin's ingenious pannabelt (1934)

There's too many busybodies now, whose knowledge of country affairs is too limited. Very often it's the people who profess to be bird lovers who are the worst. For example, some wardens have been putting goshawk eggs in sparrowhawk nests to help the rarer species make a comeback. But, of course, the bigger birds gets all the food and may later even turn on the adult. That can't be good for sparrowhawks.

Some people think grouse-keepers shoot every bird of prey in sight, but what do they know. Take the little merlin, for instance. I've always made a point of looking after these rarities and I wouldn't even let the bird people in to ring them. Many's the time I've chased them off because they do far more harm than good – tramping all over the place and the grouse nests for a start.

Up to ten years ago we always had four or five merlin nests at Byrecleugh, but not now as these sensitive birds are harried by birdy people. Now there are only one or two pairs here. Do you know, I used to take the young merlins little presents – a vole or mouse which I would skin and gut and feed to the nestlings in little pieces.

However, we have far more falcons now. And we never used to see a harrier, but they're spreading like wildfire. The crow population is still a major threat, but there's no way you could get them down without reverting to alphachloralose.

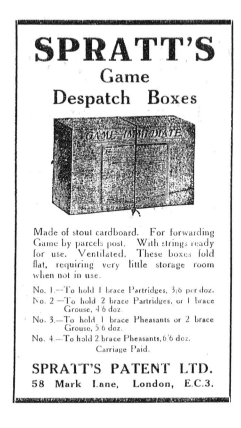

Spratt's game despatch boxes (1935)

Filling up the panniers (1939)

Poaching was not much of a problem till about ten years ago – then came the lurcher boys. They used to get hopelessly lost on the estate, but now they have the access roads and pylons to guide them. The factor told me to shoot their dogs, but I asked who would pay my fines if caught. Now they don't seem to prosecute anyone – they're all afraid of these bloody roughs bombing their homes or beating them up.

Willie's retirement bungalow is peacefully situated in the countryside, not far from his birthplace at Duns.

I wouldn't go to Floors to retire – everyone there is expected to help out with the pheasants. Not me. No, I've had the best of it.

That said, I think Willie will agree that we still have many very fine grouse-keepers throughout the country. Their contribution to our sport is immeasurable and I just wish that novice Guns were more appreciative of their dedication. On moors where two teams of beaters are used, the keeper in charge of the first lot must take his lunch

Overleaf: The keepers of Gunnerside break for lunch

at an inconvenient time, so that he can muster his men for the first drive after lunch. Although this is no great hardship, he does miss the splendid conviviality at the lunch hut. And although he may complete his duties earlier than the others, he still has to hang around till the end of the day, to help pick-up and make himself generally useful.

On some moors guests arrive and depart every week, or even more frequently, after the Twelfth, and the headkeeper has to receive all their gear into the gunroom, find and delegate loaders for most of them, and make sure that a suitable number of cartridges are available. His head will be buzzing with worries about the beaters – will they all turn up and are they sufficiently experienced? Are there enough pickers-up and has everyone's lunch been organised? Will the weather be kind, will the new drive be satisfactory, is there sufficient transport? What's to be done if the Colonel is dangerous again, and can I rely on the boss to get the Guns going after lunch?

In the weeks leading up to the Twelfth, the headkeeper will be increasingly worried about the number of birds. Even in a good year the day's success depends on his skilful organisation and order of the drives. He is the one who has given all the underkeepers their concise instructions, he is the one who has hired all the assistants and he is the one who must ensure that everyone is punctual at the appropriate rendezvous.

Even when shooting is over for the day, the headkeeper has much to do. He must ensure that the game is properly stored or despatched to the dealer's, that departing guests are each given a brace, that their guns are cleaned and all the vehicles are in good order. The dogs must be fed and cleaned, and plans for the following day reassessed in the light of the latest weather forecast and the present day's experiences.

Fortunately, on most moors the headkeeper is not alone in his demanding role as game manager, personnel officer and diplomat. Nowadays more and more owners are keen to share this onerous burden of responsibility, and not only where they have a vested interest in a commercial operation. Proprietors of moors are increasingly interested in maximising the potential of their land, to have successful profit-making operations such as farming and forestry, but at the same time be sympathetic to wildlife and landscape and provide quality shooting.

An important step forward was taken with the formation of the Moorland Gamekeepers' Association in 1987. Before this many grouse-keepers had felt rather isolated, so it was not surprising that so many of them leapt at the chance to join the new representative body. Now, at regular meetings, they can draw on each other's experiences in discussing matters such as continuing habitat loss through over-grazing, and formulate joint plans for remedial action. Much of their energy is channelled through area committees, such as those representing the North Yorkshire Moors, South Pennines and Derbyshire Moors, to address regional as well as national problems.

Grouse-keeping has certainly come a long way since Willie Veitch started out between the wars. In many ways science and technology have made the job easier, but on the other hand the keeper is increasingly regarded as a custodian of the countryside and is forced to accommodate wide-ranging interests. If he is to survive and prosper into the next century he must bend with the wind of change which rarely stops blowing between the butts.

9

A Natural History

The red grouse is very special in that it is our only gamebird which is shot in very large numbers without being the subject of rearing and release. Several million acres remain devoted to its preservation, so, because its habitat is largely restricted to the heather moors of the north and west, it is true to say that it holds the balance of power in upland conservation. Its welfare is the concern of both sportsman and conservationist, whose increasingly close co-operation is essential in securing the fragile upland ecosystem for a whole range of protected species as well as game.

The early history of the red grouse was detailed in Chapter 1. Suffice to say, the large numbers we have now are almost entirely due to the activities of man, both in the promotion of sport and the fortuitous or deliberate alteration or destruction of habitat. In most ways this makes little or no difference to the species' natural history, but when it comes to distribution and population it is another matter. Whatever is said of decline, we are always talking only relatively and the fact is that this species remains at an artificially high population level in a country that was originally well wooded and provided far less suitable habitat.

Because of the tremendous interest in the grouse as a gamebird, for both sporting and economic reasons, it has been the subject of an exceptional amount of study, the chief aim of which, to put it crudely, has been to discover how to 'grow' more. Such immense detail must remain the focus of more specialised volumes.

Range and Habitat

The red grouse is a subspecies (race), *Lagopus lagopus scoticus*, of the willow grouse, which ranges widely across America and Eurasia. Its distinctive markings once led ornithologists to believe that it was a separate species. Whereas other willow grouse have white wings all year, and white body plumage in winter, the red grouse has no need to change to winter white in Britain's relatively mild climate. No doubt the plumage difference has been accelerated by long island isolation, but the presence of an intermediate form, *L. variegatus*, in west Norway suggests that speciation is not complete. It has been suggested that *L.l. scoticus* is halfway towards specific differentiation.

Red grouse are confined to northern and western Britain and Ireland, where their year-round distribution on treeless moorland closely mirrors areas of abundance of their main food plant, ling heather. Grouse moors are mostly at an altitude of 300–600m (980–1,970ft), but they also occur from sea level to about 900m (2,950ft), as heather occurs at different heights in different areas. Much of the current range was

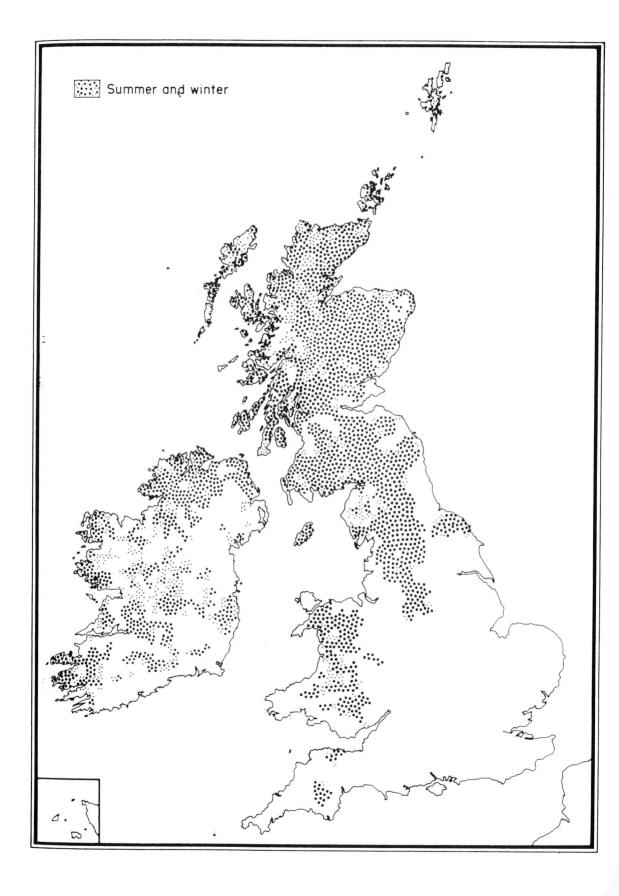

once forest and scrub, but regeneration of trees is prevented by burning and grazing, to sustain grouse-shooting or farming, or both.

The Scottish Highlands have long been the grouse's stronghold, the drier east being especially important, but in north-east England birds are equally abundant, though over a smaller area. In the west, where it is wetter, the heather does not do so well and there are generally fewer birds. Density is also determined by the nature of the underlying rock, numbers being highest over base-rich rocks such as diorite, epidiorite and all limestones, which increase soil fertility and therefore the nutritional value of the heather. The best ground may hold 50–60 pairs per sq km (0.39 sq miles) – as high as achieved on most managed moors, though 100 pairs may be achieved in exceptional years in the east. The lowest natural densities are over granite or thick peat, which is more acid. Therefore numbers are generally low in Ireland, where a few birds still occur in mountain regions, and on western boglands, where there is little attempt at habitat management or vermin control. Decline has been marked in Ireland since 1920, though reasons are unclear.

Scotland has about 800,000ha (2 million acres) of heather moorland suitable for grouse, but much of this remains under threat from afforestation, over-grazing (especially by sheep and deer), and even tourism. Nonetheless, the red grouse remains the most widespread of gamebirds north of the border, breeding in every mainland county and all island groups. There are good populations in the Borders, the Outer Hebrides (most abundant on Lewis, quite common on Harris and North Uist, and scarce or absent from Benbecula southwards), and Orkney (breeding on most islands from Roussay south, though not on the northern isles), where the suitable area is steadily shrinking as more land is cultivated. They also breed on all the main Inner Hebridean islands other than Coll and Tiree, and in Shetland the small population (reintroduced 4 May, 1989) is confined to the mainland.

Wales has a scattering of reasonable moors, but much has been lost to afforestation and piecemeal destruction of habitat. And, as in Ireland, there has been insufficient vermin control, isolated moors being particularly susceptible to rapid recolonisation by foxes.

England and Wales now struggle to preserve about 400,000ha (1 million acres) of heather moorland. England's main centres of population are confined to the north, notably along the Pennines from Derbyshire to the Scottish border, on the Yorkshire moors and in parts of the Lake District. There are also good moors in parts of Northumberland, Durham, Cumbria and the Bowland Fells (Lancashire). Other than that, there is but a sprinkling of birds on the English side of the Welsh border (predominantly Shropshire), and tiny remnant populations on Exmoor and Dartmoor. The 1820–25 reintroductions there failed, but those on Dartmoor in 1915–16 succeeded. Other unsuccessful reintroductions were those to Bagshot Heath, Surrey in 1871, and the heaths of Suffolk and Norfolk—Brandon 1854, Elveden 1864–5 and Sandringham 1878.

Red grouse – summer/winter distribution in the British Isles (from Sporting Birds of the British Isles *by Brian P. Martin, published by David & Charles)*

Grouse are occasionally seen outside their normal range, but these are almost always birds temporarily displaced by exceptional weather. Some sightings involve confusion with the dark-brown (*montana*) phase of the grey partridge. However, it should not be assumed that the red grouse is confined to heather-dominated moorland, bog and rough grazing. Some breed on raised bogs and on several coastal sand-dune heaths such as the Sands of Forvie (Grampian), but others on small patches of heather surrounded by arable land or woodland seem unable to maintain viable populations for long. The degree to which birds are able to survive and breed in areas with relatively little heather also depends on the availability of desirable alternative foods, such as crowberry and bilberry.

Thus the red grouse is an interesting example of a species whose distribution depends on a multiplicity of factors, ranging from the effect of underlying rock on the nutritive value of food plants to climate and disturbance. Moor management is the key to high population density. This involves control of predators, especially foxes and crows, drainage where waterlogging exists, provision of grit to aid digestion, occasional application of fertilisers, suppression of invasive vegetation such as scrub and bracken, strict control of grazing and, above all, rotational burning of heather to provide a continuous succession of young heather shoots for food, to control the heather beetle and suppress grouse disease. At the same time some old heather must be left for shelter and nesting.

Population and Bag

After the last ice-age, and long before man had any significant impact on the environment, much of Britain, including the north, was covered in woodland, up to about 600m (1,970ft) above sea level. Then there were relatively few areas of moorland and it is likely that the red grouse was confined to the moorland edge along the tree-line and to clearings within the woodland. Numbers were undoubtedly very low and the population probably remained very stable until, about 5,000 years ago, man settled in northern Britain and started to clear the trees to make way for crops and livestock. Later the demand for timber grew equally rapidly and eventually most of our woodlands were lost. Sheep stocks increased dramatically in the eighteenth and nineteenth centuries and their grazing on moorlands helped to create vast new areas of habitat suitable for grouse. Ironically, we are now fighting to preserve this man-made habitat, which holds grouse at an unnaturally high level.

Willow grouse populations always fluctuate quite widely on a cyclical basis, Britain's tending to revolve around a six- or seven-year cycle. Many factors affect the population dynamics, and as these are all constantly changing it is difficult to suggest anything like an accurate population level. Nonetheless, Watson suggested a breeding population of under 500,000 pairs for the whole of the British Isles in 1976. This reflected general decline since World War I, as borne out by bag records. In 1911 Leslie estimated the average annual bag for England, Scotland and Wales together at 2.5 million birds, and it is likely that a further half million were shot in Ireland. In 1983 Harradine estimated the total bag for the British Isles at only 260,000–660,000. The main causes of decline are poorer moor management through a dramatic reduction

Bracken – one scourge of the grouse moors (The Game Conservancy)

in the number of keepers, overgrazing, increasing incidence of disease, increased predation and loss of habitat.

Grouse are generally short-lived. Nearly two out of three alive in August die within a year, irrespective of shooting. Annual mortality averages 65 per cent so that most nest just once. Some may live for eight years. A moor's breeding population is determined by the number of cocks holding territories. Birds without territories are driven into marginal areas where, progressively weakened through hunger and exposed to predators, they soon die. Grouse are non-dispersive (80–90 per cent die within about a mile of where ringed) so the surplus fails to move to other moors and is eliminated by April. In most years the maxim is to shoot hard and early to bag as many of the *surplus* grouse as possible before packing and severe weather make them much more difficult to shoot. They will die anyway.

Numbers fluctuate widely in all areas, commonly three- to five-fold and occasionally more than ten-fold. Bags per unit area have generally been higher in England than in Scotland or Wales, probably a reflection of heather quality (determined by underlying rock and management practices) and shooting pressure.

Description and Identification

This small-headed, rotund gamebird is easy to identify and there are few species with which it may be confused in the upland habitat. Sometimes the upper parts of its range overlap with those of the ptarmigan, but the latter is about 10 per cent smaller and has permanently white wings and underparts. Larger male red grouse may approach the size of a female black grouse (the greyhen), but the latter is greyer, is the only British gamebird with a forked tail and has a pale wing-bar.

Flight is fast, birds generally hugging the contours of the land, with bursts of rapid, rather mechanical wing-beats alternating with glides on downcurved wings. The main colours are a deep vinaceous brown in the male and tawny brown in the female, though the sexes are not very different. However, there are considerable regional, seasonal and individual variations in plumage colour. Among the most distinctive are the generally paler Irish and Hebridean birds, once regarded by some authorities as a separate race, *Lagopus hibernicus*, but this has been discounted as hibernian birds have a different moulting pattern and feather growth in milder western areas. In addition, the identity of Irish birds has been confused by numerous introductions of English and Scottish birds. The *scoticus* subspecies was identified by Latham in 1787.

Hybrids with black grouse and ptarmigan have been recorded.

Adult Male
Average length: 38–42cm (15–16.5in)
Tail 8–9cm (3–3.5in)
Wing span: 55–66cm (21.5–26in)
Average weight: 680g (1lb 8oz) (at start of shooting season) within a range 600–908g
   (1lb 5oz–2lb).

Many authors have recorded both smaller and larger birds and attributed such to regional variations, but reliable statistical analysis is scant. For example, it has been said that those of Yorkshire are the smallest, but Daniel, in his *Rural Sports*, mentioned one killed, near Richmond, which weighed 25oz (709g). Pennant recorded one of 29oz (822g), Morris one of 30oz (850g) in Wales and one of 31oz (879g) near Todmorden in Lancashire. Harting (1901) said the grouse in Orkney were thought to exceed in weight those found in any part of Scotland. He gave the Scottish mainland best as 28oz (794g), compared with 30oz (850g) for Orkney. And, 'In England on Alston moors, old hens weigh 23oz, old cocks 26oz; in Upper Swaledale 28–30oz.'

The bill is brownish-black, half hidden by feathers: there are a few small white feathers at the base, ending in a thread of white on the side of the head. The iris is

Hen grouse caught in late June and in poor condition, with a prominent keel and unable to fly (The Game Conservancy)

chestnut brown, the feathers of the eyelids white and the membrane over the eyebrows (the comb) large and red (the female's is smaller and pinker). The comb is more prominent in birds with higher social rank. The head feathers are deep chestnut brown; the crown irregularly barred in summer with brownish black, as is the neck on the back and nape. The chin, throat and breast are reddish chestnut brown, the breast blacker in the middle, the chestnut bars being narrower than the black ones, and some of the feathers are white at their tips; the ground colour paler, and more barred in summer. The back is red brown, minutely barred with brownish black, most of the feathers having also a patch of black.

The wing-coverts are reddish chestnut brown barred black, the ten primaries dusky brown and the fifteen secondaries mostly dusky brown. Their outer margins are minutely mottled with reddish brown, and the inner five reddish brown minutely barred with brownish black, and with patches of black. The tertiaries are also brown, edged on the outside and freckled with lighter brown. The greater and lesser underwing-coverts are white, occasionally spotted and barred with brown. The short, straight tail of sixteen feathers is slightly rounded. The under-tail coverts are chestnut with a black bar, and the end and the tips white.

The legs are feathered, grey-white, sometimes mottled brown. The toes, too, are feathered (longer in winter to facilitate walking on snow), also grey-white. The first toe is extremely short, the third the longest, the fourth a little longer than the second. They are roughened underneath and the front ones webbed at the base, and with three plates at the end. The claws are rather long, arched, flattened and with blunt tips; they are blackish brown at the base and greyish yellow at the end. The bird's Latin name: *Lagopus* (hare-footed) is equally appropriate as descriptive of its thickly clothed foot and its fleetness as a runner.

The male is in summer plumage from the end of May or the beginning of June to the beginning of October and in winter plumage from mid-October to mid-May. He is in eclipse from the end of May into June. Unlike other races of willow grouse, *scoticus* never has white wings, but adults often appear slightly greyer in winter, when many Scottish birds show distinct white barring and white patches on the flanks and belly.

Adult Female
Average length: 34–36cm (13.25–14.25in)
Tail 7–8cm (2.75–3in)
Wing span: 52–63.5cm (20.5–25in)
Average weight: 586g (1lb 4½oz) within a range 550–670g (1lb 3½oz–1lb 7½oz)

The female is about 5 per cent smaller than the male, generally less bulky, and paler. She is more heavily barred with lighter pigment whereas he has thinner, more wavy lines and spots. She also has more brown and yellow mottling on the wings and dark tail. Her white feathers at the base of the bill are duller. The iris is hazel and the comb over the eye smaller and duller.

The head, crown, back of neck and nape are yellowish chestnut brown, tinged with red with a few black spots, all paler in summer. The chin, throat and breast are pale brownish red barred with brownish black, tipped yellowish, and paler in summer. The sides are barred with black and yellowish; the back yellowish chestnut brown tinged with red, paler in summer, the tips of most of the feathers yellowish.

The greater and lesser wing-coverts are barred black and tipped yellowish. The primaries, secondaries and tertiaries are paler brown, more tinged with grey; greater and lesser underwing-coverts mostly white, but some brown and others barred.

The four middle tail feathers are barred with black and tipped yellowish, the rest barred with reddish, except towards the tips, which are yellowish grey. The upper tail coverts are barred black and tipped yellowish.

The female is generally in summer plumage from April to August and winter plumage from August to March. However, as with the male, the timing of moult is subject to considerable individual variation, diseased birds moulting later.

Juvenile

At first the young are covered with pale, yellowish-grey down; the head chestnut, edged with darker brown. The lower parts are mottled with pale brown and the upper parts with deep brown.

After a month the bill is brownish black and the tip of the upper mandible whitish. The iris is hazel. The head, crown, back of neck and nape are brownish black, each feather edged and barred with yellowish red; the neck on the sides and in front, greyish yellow. The throat is greyish yellow and the breast is yellowish grey, barred with brownish black; back, brownish black, each feather edged and barred with yellowish red. The primaries, secondaries and tertiaries have the outer webs greyish brown, irregularly edged and barred with pale reddish yellow. The legs are yellowish grey and the claws pale brown.

When fully fledged, the young resemble the adult female. The head, crown, back of neck and nape are pale yellowish red, barred with blackish brown; chin, throat and breast, paler. The back is pale yellowish red, mottled and barred with brownish black and pale yellow, most of the feathers having a small whitish spot at the tip. The primaries, secondaries and tertiaries are greyish brown barred with greyish yellow, as is the tail. The comb is less distinctive. Cocks have chestnut under the chin and on the throat, with little or no black barring, while in the hen these feathers are generally yellower and the black barring is more pronounced.

At 11–12 weeks old, the young grouse cannot be distinguished from the old at long distance, but at close range look for the arrow-shaped, light bands on the back (transverse bands in old birds).

Ageing and Sexing Grouse

Because the red grouse is a highly prized table bird and the young always fetch much higher prices, it is economically important to separate young from old. Hosts generally like to give their guests a brace of young birds each, and discovering the proportion of young in the bag helps to show which areas of a moor have been most productive.

In the old days many inaccurate methods for ageing grouse were used. Some people

Plumage – upper: summer flank feathers of a hen grouse (left) and a cock (right); lower: corresponding winter feathers of a hen (left) and a cock (right). Note the more barred effect in the hen, especially in summer plumage (The Game Conservancy)

thought that if they held a grouse up by its lower jaw, and the jaw broke, then that was a young bird, but this can fail with advanced birds – even on 12 August – and within a few weeks of the season opening proves hopeless.

Identifying a young bird by testing the strength of the breastbone or skull, usually by crushing it with the thumb, is unreliable, even on 12 August if the young are advanced. Some people point to the relatively short third-outermost primary (main wing feather) of the young bird, but with well-developed young (sometimes by early August, and certainly by late August in most years) this no longer shows. Further confusion arises in that some old birds which moult late (particularly late-nesting hens) can also have a relatively short third primary, because the two outermost from the previous year remain unshed while the third is still growing.

Therefore the simplest and most reasonably accurate way to identify young grouse is to examine the shape of the two outermost primaries. In an old bird these have rounded ends, whereas in a young one they are pointed in comparison with the other primaries, and sometimes have tiny, gingery spots. However, a second-year bird that has not yet moulted still has these two feathers pointed, but they will be tattered and of a faded gingery-brown colour. A bird whose outermost primary is still growing, with a flaky, grey sheath at the base and the third-outermost primary apparently fully grown, is definitely old.

Further clues are gained from the feet. An old toe-nail which is becoming detached means an old bird because mature birds shed their toe-nails from July to September. The old bird's scar across the top of the new nail, indicating where the old one was attached, may be visible for weeks. An old bird's new claws are blunter and thicker, with slight transverse corrugations, but a young bird's claws are long, sharp and smooth.

One other unfailing method is to look for the bursa – the blind pouch just inside the vent, projecting into the abdomen. That of a young grouse is pronounced – about 8–18mm ($\frac{5}{18}$–$1\frac{1}{16}$in) long, but old birds have no bursa at all.

Voice

If any sound epitomises wild heather moorland, it must be the call of the red grouse, popularly rendered as *go-back, go-back*, that voice of defiance, or of alarm to mate and young. It is heard at all times of day, from before sunrise until after sunset. There is also a repeated *kow-ok-ok-ok*. The cock's crow, a loud, clear *cok-ok-ok*, is especially noticeable during courtship and early in the morning. Altogether, sixteen calls have been recognised in adults, those of the female being higher pitched. The duration and volume of some calls vary with the rank of the individual bird, being most intense during the male's display at the boundary of his territory.

Breeding

It is inevitable that the breeding cycle of the red grouse should attract great interest because the bird's numbers fluctuate widely and it is numbers which are most important in the commercialisation of grouse-shooting. Research continues into ways to boost 'production', or at least achieve some consistency of bags, but these notes are largely confined to the species' natural reproduction.

Introductions, Rearing and Release

As already mentioned, adult grouse have been captured and subsequently released elsewhere in attempts to re-establish them in lost territory, to increase their range or to boost flagging stocks. This has met with little success. Bags may have increased soon after release, but not in subsequent seasons. Grouse scarcity is not the result of loss of vigour among local birds and it is undoubtedly a waste of time and money to introduce birds from well-stocked moors. Attention should focus on effective habitat management and predator control, never forgetting that less-favoured moors will never be able to yield the same number of brace per acre as those with optimum habitat.

Some introductions have been preposterously optimistic. Even though grouse thrive under widely different climate, vegetation, altitude and topography, individual populations become adapted to local conditions and do not take kindly to being uprooted. For example, birds used to the specific nutrient intake of a dry moor over limestone in north-east Scotland are bound to suffer if released onto an acid bog in the wet west of Ireland. And apart from chemical considerations, there are physical problems in that birds from a region with relatively dark plumage will find camouflage difficult where paler feathers are more suitable. No doubt the intruders will also feel out of place and thus be stressed.

That said, introductions of red grouse to the Ardennes district of Belgium and the Eifel district of West Germany, from 1886, met with partial success. By the early twentieth century there were about a thousand birds on both sides of the border, but since 1950 records have been only sporadic in Germany, and in 1972 the Belgian stock was estimated at only about ten pairs. There are many examples of grouse happily living in domestication. One lived for six years in captivity at Wilton House, Blackburn, and in 1898 Mr Assheton-Smith had a tame covey at Vaynol. Other tame grouse are said to have bred with wild grouse and then returned to those who cared for them. Some 'free-range' birds have become as tame as pet dogs and even pugnaciously try to see off intruders, be they canine or human.

Grouse will certainly breed reasonably well in captivity, but are totally unsuited to major rearing-and-release schemes: even the most carefully orchestrated have given little benefit. After being fed on highly nutritious crumbs, like those fed to young pheasants, partridges and turkeys, plus a supplement of heather, young grouse cannot adapt to a wild diet. Their digestion of the tough, all-heather diet is poor because their blind guts have become too short and their gizzards too small and soft. Although a few may survive, most will die within a few days of release.

Released birds are also less able to fend for themselves. Aggressive, territorial birds will drive them from the heather, onto marginal land or farmland, where they soon starve to death. In addition, they are naïve when it comes to predators and soon succumb to stoats, foxes and birds of prey. The few which survive all this are generally so tame they are rarely a sporting quarry.

Some rearing methods have been slightly more successful, in allowing chicks free run on heather within coops before release, but these are so labour intensive they are not economic, and predation remains a major problem.

Territories, Pairing and Courtship

Although red grouse may be legally shot up to 10 December, it is desirable that the main cull is complete by the end of October, ideally earlier, so that there is minimal interference with the birds' establishment of territories. Territorial behaviour appears to limit the species' population and determine whether a male will reproduce or not. Males without territories do not court females and do not usually survive for long. Pair formation, courtship, copulation, nesting and almost all feeding (at least until hatching) occur within the breeding territory, so it is important that the territory contains the diversity of habitat types to support these activities. This is best achieved by managing the heather to provide a good variety of plant ages within a few acres.

The species is generally monogamous, but a few males with large territories may hold two females which both nest within his patch. Very occasionally a male may associate with three or more females but meets with little success. Usually, there is at

In sorting old from young grouse, comparison of primary-feather length is useful

least a small excess of males, which means that even some territorial males fail to get mates. Both male and female are sexually mature in their first year, when all the females generally pair, as well as many males, providing territories are obtained. A territory usually covers 1–12ha (2.5–30 acres) but an unpaired male may need as little as 0.2ha (0.5 acres) and a pair 0.3ha (0.75 acres). In western Ireland males can hold up to 50ha (125 acres).

Cocks become more noisy and aggressive in August and, exceptionally, pairing may take place in August and September, when young birds involved are only 3–5months old. However, associations are more tenuous during autumn and early winter, when females may remain in a territory only spasmodically, many females moving from male to male before forming a firm bond, usually from February onwards. Once consolidated, a pair bond may last two or more years, always depending on the male's success in holding territory each autumn. If he fails to take territory the bond is immediately broken, even if both birds somehow manage to survive. If the male dies – perhaps through shooting – the female will associate with another male on a nearby territory, even in the spring. In the critical month of October many pairs change around and territories alter.

During the first half of the winter, birds are on their territories for only short periods, notably on fine mornings, when they are seen proclaiming their rights from boulders or walls. But as winter advances birds become increasingly territorial and towards the end of the season often remain on their territories all day, in pairs, allowing no afternoon feeding by intruders. Meanwhile, old males that have lost their territories, and young males that have failed to establish territories, remain in packs and suffer a high mortality through keen competition for meagre food supplies. Although grouse eat less than 10 per cent of available food in their territories, they select shoots rich in phosphorous and nitrogen, and it is likely that an important factor in territory defence is securing a good supply of nutrients for the female in egg-production.

Territories are usually fairly evenly distributed on heather moorland and occupy all suitable habitat. But high grouse density reduces territory size and makes it more difficult for surplus birds to establish territory. However, the better the moor is managed and the more favourable the weather and habitat, the better the food supply and the smaller the area needed to maintain territory holders in healthy condition. That said, there may also be some correlation between territory spacing and reduction of predation. If snow completely covers feeding areas, birds squeeze onto the nearest clear ground, where they establish temporary territories, and return to original territories when the thaw comes.

It is the older males which are the first to establish themselves in the autumn,

Headkeeper paying the helpers at Gunnerside. Such overheads can be very considerable indeed

Earl Peel takes a grouse from one of his labradors, watched by Lady Peel on their Gunnerside Moor, Yorkshire

Overleaf: *Ready for action at beautiful Byrecleugh, in the Borders*

maintaining or enlarging their territories from the previous season. Later, first-year males begin to take over unoccupied patches and try to establish new territories between existing ones. Others try to oust older males. Those without territories are forced into marginal areas, where most die chiefly through starvation, predation and disease. The handful of survivors will breed only if they are lucky enough to take over a territory on the death of the owner. Males without mates may also occupy territories and feed almost entirely within them.

The dramatic way in which the male marks his territory often surprises and may even startle moorland visitors. In exceptional cases a bird will physically attack a person: in October, 1989 one actually clung to a walker's clothing. But generally the display is confined to leaping skyward with wings spread, to descend steeply, extending the neck and feet and fanning the tail. Courtship displays are mostly similar to antagonistic ones, the advertising behaviour of the unpaired male in his territory serving to attract unpaired females as well as warn off other males. During such activity, the male's red head comb is very prominent, dilating and even projecting above the crown when fully erected. The female's smaller, pinker combs can also be erected.

When a female adopts a submissive posture the male's threatening display is modified to courtship display, which takes up only a small part of their time. This consists largely of strutting and waltzing, wing-drooping and tail-fanning, rapid stamping and bowing, and head-waggling. Females are attracted to more vigorous males.

Nest, Eggs and Incubation

The hen makes a simple, shallow scrape in the ground, scantily lining it with vegetation, chiefly grass and heather, occasionally small pieces of peat. Favourite sites are in the safety of deep, old, heather but with recently burnt ground, producing young heather shoots for food, nearby. Most nests are partly overhung by vegetation and on hard, well-drained, flat land. However, a substantial number are either completely uncovered or completely covered. Most sites are within 150m (500ft) of grit sources, water and grassy or mossy areas where chicks can feed.

Though nesting occasionally takes place as early as the end of February during mild weather, eggs are usually laid from late April into early May. The single clutch of 6–9 (occasionally 2–17) oval, glossy eggs are creamy white, variably covered by chocolate-brown mottling and blotches, sometimes tinged red. The average size is 46 × 32mm (1.81–1.26in) within a range of 41–50 × 30–34mm (1.61–1.97 × 1.18–1.34in). Each egg weighs 25g (0.88oz). The clutch size is slightly larger on low moors and varies with density of pairs. The warmer and drier the season the larger the number of eggs. In years with high burdens of parasitic worms clutches have been

A grouse retrieved. Good gundogs greatly enhance a day's success

Strips of burnt heather at the Biddulphs' Lammermuirs shoot. Note the swiped edges, which act as firebreaks

generally small. Replacement eggs are often laid after egg loss, occasionally twice in one season, but second clutches are usually smaller. The first few eggs are laid at 36–48 hour intervals, the rest at 24 hours, at any time during daylight, and are partly covered by the female between layings. Very large clutches are sometimes the result of two females laying in the same nest. Dual incubation is known.

Incubation, by the female alone, takes about 22 days (range 19–25 days) and commences with the arrival of the last or penultimate egg. Hatching is synchronous and the shells are left in the nest. During this time the male is attentive and escorts the female to and from feeding.

A mild winter followed by late snow may cause great havoc, but grouse eggs can stand a surprising amount of cold and hens will continue sitting in fairly deep snow. Even badly frosted eggs rarely fail to hatch. Frost and snow *after hatching* are much more serious.

The downy chicks leave the nest soon after hatching, when dry, and are tended by both parents, being brooded by the female while small. They mostly feed themselves, can flutter at 7 days, fly at 12–18 days, are fully grown at 30–35 days, and in a good year become independent at about two months. In poor years they may be abandoned when just six weeks old, when some broods join together. Generally, they remain together as a family into the autumn, even as late as November. Predation of chicks is greatest during the first week, after which it steadily diminishes. Grouse are very bold in defence of their young, not only mounting distraction displays but also launching attacks on intruders. There are reports of grouse carrying their young. Generally high hatching success and a moderate rate of chick mortality are probably partly due to close care by both parents. However, hatching success has been shown to vary with clutch size. In one study, although a clutch of nine produced the greatest *proportion* of eggs hatched, it was one of eleven that yielded the greatest *number* of chicks hatched.

The male's main role both during incubation and after the chicks have hatched is to keep guard, but if the female should be killed he will take sole charge of the brood, even if newly hatched.

Diet and Feeding Behaviour

Except during the first ten days of its life, the red grouse is almost entirely herbivorous. But, unlike other races of willow grouse, it can feed almost exclusively on one plant – heather – throughout the year because snow cover is usually only patchy and light in Britain's relatively mild climate. As a result, most food is taken on the ground and only in exceptional circumstances will it feed in trees. It will also dig through snow to reach food.

There are some regional and seasonal variations, and the densities of breeding populations and breeding success appear to be related to the amount and quality of heather available. Where other plants are scarce, such as over granite, the ling heather (*Calluna vulgaris*) is the main food all year, but other foods are taken where available (especially over limestone and in summer). Where a choice exists, birds appear to ignore suitable foods in favour of more nutritious items. Because it is difficult to extract

Grouse require grit to grind up the hard fibrous heather in their gizzards. This illustration shows natural quartzite magnified two-and-a-half times (The Game Conservancy)

sufficient nutrients from the fibrous heather the grouse has an exceptionally large gizzard which contains plenty of grit to break down the food physically. In addition, it has a relatively long intestine and large pair of caeca (the caecum is the blind end of the first part of the large intestine) to improve chemical digestion and absorption of nutrients. Such specialisation is worthwhile because heather is abundant and accessible all year round.

The grouse eats heather shoots, flowers and seed-heads, adults preferring the current year's growth from heather aged about 2–4 years. It is thought that birds actively select heather richer in phosphorus and nitrogen in choosing particular parts, ages and heights of plants. Indeed, the female's success in selective feeding prior to laying is thought partly to determine breeding success. Experiments indicated that application of fertilisers to impoverished areas would boost grouse production, but results have been disappointing. The money would be better spent on heather burning.

Daily intake of heather by Scottish grouse has been measured at 50–60g (1.8–2.1oz) in winter and 60–80g (2.1–2.8oz) in captivity. In spring, heather forms about 90 per cent of the diet, with ericaceous shrubs constituting most of the rest. Grouse breeding density is increased where a systematic heather-burning programme is in operation because the young shoots encouraged are more nutritious than old ones, the *productivity* of plants being unchanged by burning.

Other vegetable matter eaten by grouse, in varying quantities according to local supply, includes: the leaves and stalks of *Vaccinium myrtillus* (the bilberry, blaeberry or whortleberry); the shoots and fruits of *Vaccinium oxycoccos* (cranberry); the flowers and shoots of *Eriophorum vaginatum* (cotton-grass or cotton sedge, sometimes called moss crop or drawmoss); *Myrica gale* (bog myrtle); *Salix herbacea* (dwarf willow); the seeds of *Juncus squarrosus* (heath rush); seeds of various grasses, buds and catkins of birch (chiefly *Betula nana*); *Rumex acetosella* (sheep's sorrel); various chickweeds; *Erica cinerea* (bell heather); *Vaccinium vitis-idaea* (cowberry); *Empetrum nigrum* (crowberry) and ripe oats on stubbles. In autumn, evidence of ground fruits in the diet can be seen in the purple-stained droppings on rocks.

Protein is especially important for chick growth, especially during the first ten days, when many invertebrates are taken, mostly flies, beetles and the larvae of sawflies. Indeed, hens are known to take chicks to areas rich in insects, such as bog flushes, and avoid young and recently burnt heather, where insects are scarce.

Experiments have shown that grouse chicks cannot grow and survive on a diet of heather alone. An additional source of protein is essential and this is likely to be insects. Generally, the more abundant the insect supply the faster the chick's growth. However, chicks also eat heather tips, moss capsules and various flowers from the first day. After three weeks the diet is virtually adult and wet summers are not so disastrous as they are for young partridges as young grouse eat far less insect food and the heather dries very quickly. Chicks also eat heather containing more nitrogen and phosphorus than that taken by adults at the same time of year.

Movements and Migration

Red grouse do not regularly migrate at certain times of year or normally travel long distances. Generally, they make only short-distance, weather-related movements, many of which are altitudinal. All grouse are highly sedentary, males more than females, though why hens are more mobile is not known. Almost all recoveries of ringed birds have been within a couple of kilometres, though females have travelled 42km (26 miles). Birds without territories are rather more mobile and are frequently forced to travel at least several kilometres into marginal areas – even light woodland – where they soon die. These surplus birds do not colonise distant areas. Grouse commonly move 1–2km (0.62–1.25 miles) to feed on oat stubbles or berries, or perhaps to drink water, particularly when in packs. Disturbed birds may travel a few kilometres ahead of beaters or an eagle.

When snow covers the heather on high ground, grouse must move downhill to feed. Surprisingly though, some move to *higher* ground during periods of heavy snow, for on the tops the wind is more likely to have drifted the snow and thus exposed the important heather. But during exceptionally severe weather, when there are light winds and the snow is deep on both high and low ground, grouse may travel quite long distances – even onto farmland – to find food. Then mortality may be very high and when most of the birds fail to return it is sometimes wrongfully assumed that they have migrated.

Notwithstanding this basically sedentary behaviour, packs have been known to move 30km (18.6 miles) or more and there have been mass movements, some over coastal waters, which have not been accounted for. Exceptionally, packs have moved several kilometres to strange territory in autumn and have not returned 'home' for several months. Generally, grouse displaced by extreme weather return home as soon as possible. In the most severe winters, such as those of 1940–41, 1946–7 and 1962–3, grouse have been encountered along roads and even in town centres, feeding on hawthorn and holly berries. One was even found in the cellar of a house in Yorkshire.

Predation and Accidents

Before the modern conservation movement got underway and protective legislation for wild birds and mammals was introduced, any moorland species thought to threaten the grouse was quickly removed, through shooting, trapping and poisoning, by a considerable army of keepers. Thus man himself quickly became the most significant predator on grouse, and as the numbers of grouse increased through careful habitat management he soon came to appreciate the importance of adequate culling to minimise the proportion of weak and diseased birds which are largely the result of overcrowding.

Today, apart from shooting, natural predation is still the main killer of grouse. However, most sportsmen now have greater understanding of the ecosystem and display great sympathy for all wildlife. Thus anyone who attempts to control predators illegally is condemned by one and all. In addition, there is greater awareness of the temporary, local nature of predation problems and many shooters try to be sparing in their control, a few preferring not to kill any predators whatsoever.

Grouse without territories suffer most from predation because they are generally weaker through inferior feeding and thus more easily caught. Also they do not know the ground so well and have little knowledge of possible escape routes. Thus few grouse are taken from May to August, when scarcely any birds without territories remain alive, but the rate of killing from September onwards, among packs of non-territorial birds, is increasingly substantial. This continues through winter and tails off in March and April.

In winter the main predators are foxes, hen harriers and golden eagles, but stoats, wild cats, sparrowhawks, peregrines and buzzards also take a few. However, their activities generally have little effect on the spring breeding-stock of good moors because the few territorial birds killed are soon replaced by non-territorial grouse. That said, exceptional concentrations of predators, such as hen harriers, on marginal ground where the grouse population is sparse, can depress the stock. In addition, winter predation slows recovery from poor breeding years. Winter predation is greater during periods of snow cover, when birds are easier to see and more concentrated.

Recent increases in grouse numbers have probably been aided by a series of unusually mild winters.

With most non-territorial birds killed by the end of May, summer predation is higher on territorial hens (incubating birds with high worm burdens emit scent which makes them more vulnerable), their eggs and young. Then the fox is the main offender, followed by harrier and eagle, with stoat, weasel and peregrine far less important. The grouse stock may be depressed where keepering is poor and predators are allowed to proliferate or where a well-run moor is surrounded by non-keepered ground so that as fast as foxes are killed others move in. In this respect, blocks of forestry pose a particular problem. In the seventies and eighties, on many Scottish moors, the number of foxes killed has been increasing at 70% per annum, crows at 5% per annum and mink at 18%!

Recent local increases in hen-harrier numbers have been causing some concern as young harriers are often fed on young grouse as well as songbirds and other small prey. However, in the absence of substantial evidence it is almost certain that some shooters exaggerate claims of harrier predation just as much as birdwatchers exaggerate claims of harrier persecution. My own opinion is that, whatever the true position, there is no way we could ever contemplate even limited, licensed shooting of any bird of prey. Most modern sportsmen would happily settle for a few less grouse and enjoy the spectacle of magnificent raptors. Commercial shooting will just have to suffer the loss and keep quiet. Many grouse eggs are taken by crows and foxes, with only a few lost to hedgehogs, deer, cattle, dogs and gulls.

Sometimes birds of prey are blamed for spoiling grouse drives by scaring the birds away, but on other occasions predators quartering neighbouring ground improve drives by concentrating grouse. Shooters should take such exceptional incidents in their stride and not look for excuses to wage war on competitive species, whether they be protected or unprotected. And all shoot-proprietors should ensure that their gamekeepers and other employees are thoroughly familiar with the law, insisting that anyone caught using poison indiscriminately and illegally will be instantly dismissed. All species should be given a little 'elbow room' on the grouse moor: after all, it is man who is the intruder there and it is he who, sometimes unwittingly, controls whatever remains of the balance of nature.

Substantial numbers of grouse are also killed accidentally, principally through collision with deer and forestry fences, and to a lesser extent through impact with overhead wires. Conservation grants now available include money to fit reflective plates to fences to reduce grouse collisions.

Other Aspects of Behaviour

Apart from the occasionally conspicuous or unusually aggressive territorial bird, few grouse reveal themselves to the hill-walker. The bird is generally loath to fly, preferring to remain inconspicuous in the heather, trusting to its cryptic colouring and stillness to avoid detection. But it is forever vigilant, peering out of cover, craning in all directions, and will run considerable distances. During courtship grouse are relatively easy to approach, but in moult they spend much time in very rank heather, for then they are more vulnerable to predators. When disturbed, they beat away low over the heather with typical gamebird whirring flight, the broad wings bowed for occasional glides before they alight again several hundred metres away. Generally, this facilitates return drives later in the day, but occasionally a pack will fly off for several kilometres and spoil subsequent sport.

After a few days' shooting in an early season, the coveys start to pack, sometimes one sex together, though that is not the general rule. By the end of August they are already more wary and wild, and in September and October getting good bags becomes increasingly difficult, with so many birds holding together and tending to come over the butts as one. Young tend to pack earlier than adults and hens more readily than cocks because it is the territory-holders which sit tight. A few old males never pack. Unattached females and non-territorial males usually group in small flocks which feed in unoccupied spaces between territories. Sometimes the homeless packs are driven from the moors by territory-holders and must resort to stubble fields, grassland, bog and scrub to feed. However, they do not usually move far and in the late morning or early afternoon the replete territory holders may allow them to return. (Males which have temporarily given up territorial behaviour have been known to form homosexual pairs in winter, for periods up to an hour or so.)

Flocking is induced by deep snow and stormy weather, but even then territorial birds are the last to join. The snowier the weather the larger the flocks, especially in areas of high population density. Packs of hundreds are not that unusual, but those over a thousand are rare. During periods of heavy snow, birds may have to keep treading to avoid being buried. They will also roost in snow, each bird scooping out a hollow when the snow is deep enough. More exceptionally, on very frosty nights, they will burrow right into powder snow. Such hollows and burrows may also be used for rest and shelter during the day to conserve energy. Otherwise, they roost in the heather or other ground vegetation, mostly communally on winter nights, less than 1m (3ft 3in) apart and sometimes in an arc facing the wind, but never so tightly as partridges. Sometimes territorial males and pairs roost on their territories in autumn and winter as well as spring, pairs settling down closer together than birds in a flock. Although most grouse go to roost soon after dusk and stir just before dawn, they are sometimes active in bright moonlight. Most roosts are on small, open sites where approaching predators may be spotted, but the majority are sheltered by nearby rocks, hillocks or vegetation. It is likely that a fresh site is used every night. In bitter weather a red grouse may awake with hoar frost on its back, yet minutes later be feeding quite happily, such is the bird's superb adaptation to its environment.

Diseases and Parasites

Although grouse disease has remained a favourite subject of the shooting press since the mid-nineteenth century (see Chapter 3), it is only since the seventies that a concerted effort has been made to do something about it. As usual, the chief spur has been money, for the shootable surplus frequently lost to disease can be considerable, and fewer birds in the bag means lower incomes for sporting estates, reduced viability for moors and the increasing risk of further habitat loss.

Not surprisingly, the two worst diseases occur most frequently on low, damp moors with high rainfall which benefits the hosts' life cycle, especially where poor management does not ensure that the heather litter – that hotbed of disease – is regularly burnt away. In the old days sportsmen spoke non-specifically of 'grouse disease', but generally alluded to the worst scourge of all, now identified as strongylosis, caused by the tiny threadworm known to scientists as *Trichostrongylus tenuis*. This parasite lives in the blind-ended part of the grouse's gut known as the caecum, whose function is not fully understood but is certainly linked with improved extraction and absorption of nutrients. The worms burrow into the gut wall, causing swelling and bleeding, so it is not surprising that they disrupt grouse nutrition, and hence survival. Because of this poor condition, affected hens lay fewer eggs and are unable to look after their chicks properly so the population is reduced. It is the latter aspect which most concerns shooters.

Birds found dead through strongylosis have emaciated breast muscles, with a prominent sternum, and others may be so weak they cannot fly. Each gut may contain 1,000–13,000 worms, visible only through a microscope or hand lens. Most grouse contain at least some worms, but birds in poor condition generally carry the most. The average worm burdens, discovered by post-mortem examination, of autumn-shot birds reflects grouse condition during the *previous* summer. Increases in worm burdens are associated with large numbers of grouse in the autumn and a mild, wet and late summer. Wet conditions promote development of the worm's infective stages.

Worm eggs lay dormant in grouse droppings during the cold of winter, but with spring warmth millions of larvae hatch and settle in the heather. They climb to the tips of the shoots and develop a tough sheath which prevents them from drying out and resists being ground up by the grit in the gizzard. Once inside the gut, the worms live off their host, mate and lay more eggs, which are excreted in droppings, thus completing the cycle. Where rainfall is over 125cm (50in) or so a year, worm burdens tend to build up and cause regular grouse population crashes every four or five years, but the larvae survival is poor on dry moors, where high worm burdens are dependent on wet summers coinciding with high grouse-population density.

For some years, scientists have sought to find a solution to this problem, but worming drugs – anthelmintics – such as those used on sheep, cattle and man for decades, are not the answer. They do not kill all the worms, nor do they need to, and reinfection soon follows. (Owners of country cats know how often worming is necessary.) The crucial point is not to allow the worm burden to reach the point at which the animal or bird starts to lose condition.

Developing drugs to contain strongylosis was simple, as was proving the efficacy of direct, oral dosing, but worming a wild grouse is not as easy as treating a tame moggie. Birds were successfully caught and dosed at night, especially pre-breeding hens, but such activities are very expensive in terms of labour and do not provide an economic solution. In any case, experiments showed that reinfection could follow quickly.

Attention turned to baits, the idea being that the grouse would dose themselves. But, in trials, the birds refused everything, preferring the monotony of heather. However, all was not lost because all grouse must take grit and, in conjunction with

Electron micrograph of strongyle worms in the gut wall of a red grouse (The Game Conservancy)

a chemical company, the Game Conservancy developed a medicated grit which the birds would accept. An anthelmintic was incorporated in kernel fat which was used as a coating on Cornish quartz grit. Monitoring of trials, which started in 1987, has shown a 44 per cent reduction in worm burdens among affected birds, and in 1989 keepers were reporting less serious grouse population crashes on moors where the drug had been used. The Game Conservancy now regards the use of medicated grit as an insurance to lower the risk of a grouse population crash, but still advises direct dosing when a crash appears imminent.

Some sportsmen believe that grouse shot in August with bare, largely unfeathered feet and legs are diseased, but this merely indicates a delayed moult through late breeding. Another misconception is that diseased birds have soft droppings, whereas such faeces, like melted chocolate, are as regular as the harder, fibrous, cylindrical ones.

The virus disease louping ill is another major problem, but more limited in range, moors in Aberdeenshire, Argyllshire, Dumfriesshire, Morayshire and parts of Perthshire being the worst affected. The disease is passed on by ticks and is well known to sheep farmers because it attacks the sheep's central nervous system, making it stagger or 'loup'. Although these ticks will attach themselves to almost any vertebrate host (hares and roe deer are prime vectors in some areas), only sheep and grouse are generally critically affected. However, the virus can persist through grouse alone, in the absence of sheep. This is particularly troublesome where the heather litter is deep, having built up where heather-burning has lapsed or the fires have been too fast and not fierce enough. As the litter depth increases, so too does the humidity within it and the tick's chances of survival there. The ticks themselves are not a threat to grouse; it is only where they carry the louping-ill virus that moor stocks can be seriously depleted. On badly infected ground, broods are frequently small and mortality high among young chicks, though some older chicks and adults die too. Poorly drained moors are especially susceptible.

Grouse are also occasionally troubled by coccidiosis, tapeworms, bacterial diseases and feather lice, but healthy, wild adults are rarely affected to a serious extent and death is generally confined to birds already weakened by other factors.

With all these problems, moor-owners should not rely on researchers to come up with 'cures'. As in so many walks of life, prevention is better, and in the case of grouse good moor management through systematic heather-burning, good grit supply and drainage, combined with adequate culling should contain most problems. But to encourage a high grouse-population density, through measures such as excessive predator control, and not to shoot enough of the surplus is to invite trouble. The ratio of healthy adults to habitat is finely balanced and no two moors are the same.

Doyens of grouse research: The Earl Peel, Dick Potts and Peter Hudson of the Game Conservancy at Gunnerside in North Yorkshire (The Game Conservancy)

10
Driving Force

A day in the butts on the Glorious Twelfth, when imagination and reminiscence intermingle

It was the Glorious Twelfth at last, and there I was, a Sassenach in bonny Scotland, home of the haggis, bagpipes, whisky, tweeds and tartans, and, above all, a million grouse. I had read all the books, bought all the right equipment, saved all my pennies, and at last I was there, slightly worried that I might do the wrong thing, but fired with enthusiasm and ready to take on the King of Gamebirds. I'd even bothered to take a few shooting lessons so that no one could accuse me of not keeping my end up, so to speak, and with a bit of luck my kills would be clean.

I knew that northern England had consistently shown better bags, and was considerably closer to my home in the south, but it had to be Scotland. Where else could the tyro go for his first expedition into grouseland? There lurked Britain's last wilderness with mile upon mile of misty mountains and an absolute ocean of heather which hitherto existed only in this southerner's subconscious.

My hotel was splendid and obviously geared up to a sporting clientele. You might say it was first class, but then I was paying the best part of £1,000 for just one day's top shooting, so why skimp on other things? It would be a real holiday!

A chum in my pheasant-shoot syndicate had encouraged me to go; he'd been tramping north for decades, stressing that it was the highlight of the year: couldn't get the honeyed heather out of his nostrils. But would he regret taking three novices north, even though we were all dabhands on partridge and pheasant, and how would we fit in with the four Americans making up the party on this let day?

Breakfast was at a leisurely 8.30am at the Heathcock Inn, where we English had booked in the night before, only a couple of miles from the grouse-moor. After our long journey by car and a boisterous night sampling every available malt, it was good to know that the day's play would not begin till 10am, but in some ways this was a bit of a fag. After all, we were used to roll-call at 9am on pheasant days, and we were rather keyed up. But at least the breakfast was good with, among other favourites, Arbroath smokies, deer liver and champagne to send us on our merry way. I wondered if the Americans were faring so well as guests of the Duke. Apparently His Grace found entertaining to be quite lucrative.

At 9.15am the sporting agent arrived in a Range Rover to whisk us off to the moorland rendezvous. 'How was the journey? Was the hotel satisfactory? Did we have wet-weather gear?' 'Fine, yes, yes', we chirruped to a man. He wasn't going to catch me out; I'd read the books: I knew how quickly this glorious day might be swallowed up by the rainstorms which brew from nothing on the tops.

When we left the public road we seemed to drive forever over sheep and cattle grids and sleeping policemen, through farmyards and floods and around tortuous bends before our rendezvous swung into sight. We could spot the Americans a mile off, with their top-quality, pristine clothing. Two looked as if they'd gone straight to Holland & Holland for instant outfitting after stepping off Concorde. One of them even had heavy Royal Hunter wellies on! Surely any fool knew that rubber boots were totally inappropriate for the moor: they make your feet sweat and do not give the support of stout, well-broken leather footwear. A third American displayed great desire to hark back to British roots. He, Irwin D. Wasserberg the Third, was actually wearing a kilt and tam-o'-shanter, and sported a dirk in his stocking. But at least the fourth man looked like an old campaigner, with his polished brogues, stockings, plus-twos and gently weathered look. Sadly, at the time I had a typically biassed English view of our ex-colonial cousins, but I was soon to learn how charming they can be and how their enthusiasm for all forms of 'hunting' more often than not puts ours in the shade. Now I always look forward to sharing their frankness and openness.

We arrived at the same time as a whole fleet of assorted cross-country vehicles – Land-Rovers, various Japanese 4×4s and a rather posh, plum-coloured Range Rover with personalised registration. Then, as one, they seemed to erupt, vehicles designed to carry five people in comfort spilling jolly groups of up to eight onto the track. Immediately there was a flurry of introductions and renewing of friendships as one more season sprang to life in this distinguished moor's 160-year shooting history. Rather appropriately, a grouse called *go-back, go-back* from a nearby knoll.

This bustling, waxproofed and tweedy army comprised keepers, loaders and pickers-up, as well as us Guns – immediately recognised by our sparkling appearance and self-satisfied grins – and a sprinkling of wives and chums along for a jolly. But there was no mistaking the air of excitement and expectation, made all the more intense by a seething mass of labradors and springer spaniels, all of which seemed to share the significance of the day.

Also in the yard were a number of muddier 4×4s, and a selection of estates and saloons, some of which had seen better days and appeared to be held together by a combination of luck and labels proclaiming either membership of various fieldsports associations and societies or stickers suggesting where 'antis' could 'get off'. This was the transport of the first beating team who, along with a couple of the underkeepers, had long since left to bring in the first drive. We certainly had the feeling that we were part of a well-practised military operation, but confidence was high and our leaders seemed to know what they were about. After all, Fred had been coming here for years and he knows when he's on to a winner. Shoots which fail to produce both quality and projected bags soon lose custom. Wise Guns go by recommendation.

On this occasion Fred had already told us the form, but, quite rightly, the agent addressed the assembled company, outlining the day's programme and, most importantly, stressing the need for the highest standards of safety in this potentially very dangerous sport. No ground game was to be shot even though hares were abundant, the reason being that in the excitement of swinging after one it is all too

Eley advertisement (1928)

easy to forget where the gun is pointing. In any case, who wants to shoot hares when grouse are on offer: total concentration is needed for these winged wonders.

There would be no shooting in front after the keeper sounded his horn to warn that the beaters were approaching, but between then and the end of the drive – indicated by a further two blasts on the horn – Guns could shoot behind at going-away birds. Obviously, anyone attempting this should not swing through the line, across his neighbours. This needs very careful watching on a grouse-moor, especially where the line of butts is not perfectly straight. Indeed, some batteries are at different levels on hilly ground and pose additional hazards. The answer is to point the gun muzzle towards the sky while turning, and as an extra safety measure a stick can be placed at each side of the butt to indicate the safe arc of fire.

Guns should be 'broken', ie open, or in their slips at all times except during drives. In this case we were relieved of the burden of even carrying our weapons as we were each assigned a loader – very experienced men, mostly keepers, from other estates. We would have to rely on them a lot because ideally a Gun should have his own regular loader, the team having practised to perfection. But none of us was wealthy enough or shot double guns frequently enough to make this worthwhile. That said, most total strangers make reasonable duos, and wherever possible regular visitors are assigned the same man, soon getting to know each other's ways.

So off we went, fully briefed. But if the drive to the lodge seemed long, that to the

Even on driven shoots the Guns must be prepared for some arduous walking to the butts

first line of butts was interminable, the convoy snaking slowly around the hillsides. Even these state-of-the-art off-roaders were hard pressed to soften the rocky way. No wonder they had to start so much earlier in the old days, when there were no access roads across the moor and Guns went by pony. But of course we made it, having traversed apparently impossible gulleys and gradients, and all the while we gently got to know each other. The Americans seemed to have shot everything on offer all over the world, including the game on their own ranches, but even for them the glorious grouse surpassed all. The seasoned campaigner, who turned out to be the leader of their group, told me in no uncertain terms that the grouse is 'the sportiest gamebird which lives in great country where great Shots become very humble. It's the best shooting there is.' No Colts for him: he was packing a pair of Holland & Hollands.

The weather was pleasantly dry and bright after recent heavy rain, but there was a strong, gusty wind in which the birds could perform well. However, there was little time to admire the scenery as we marched straight off to the first butts. There we had another short briefing to explain what was expected to happen and to re-emphasise the need for safety. We also drew for positions. The agent produced what appeared to be a swish silver cartridge, but when he turned the end out popped eight numbered slips, which we selected at random. It was important that we remembered these numbers because at each drive we would all move up two positions, in the customary attempt to make sure that everyone has a fair share of the shooting. I was number 6, so on the second drive I would be 8, on the third 2, and so on.

On some private shoots the owners prefer to place all the Guns on all the drives so that there is no question of anyone missing out. After all, you cannot guarantee anything, even when a particular drive is well established. But such placing is rare nowadays because few shoots remain in the control of one man. Most landowners have been compelled to form syndicates, to share the enormous costs, and then some form of non-preferential stand selection is essential. However, there is nothing to stop a syndicate making sure that a guest draws the number which is likely to provide the best sport, given the conditions and order of drives on the day. Generally the central numbers provide most action, but with, say, a shift of wind one of the flanking Guns can suddenly find himself in the hotseat.

On the first drive the butts were well strung out up the hillside and number 6 was one of the more distant ones, but who can object to a sapping tramp through the heather when the surroundings are so inspirational? In any case, the more elderly and feeble among us could always hitch a lift in the Snowcat or little Argocat, a wonderful invention. So we trudged stoically on, men whose business lives revolved chiefly around sitting for long periods now enjoying the novelty of real exercise. But there was no way this lot could contemplate walking-up grouse without a course in the gym.

After leaving companions at their allotted stations and wishing them good luck (how dare I presume they needed it!), I was eventually ensconced in my heather-topped castle, from where it seemed as if I could survey the entire kingdom of the grouse. When the action began it would be more like a gun turret on a warship, but to begin with it was a place of perfect peace. Now I was to discover that driven grouse shooting consists largely of long periods of waiting punctuated by bursts of immensely

Provision of suitable stiles and stream bridges help the day run smoothly

exciting activity, when success comes only through fine co-ordination of senses and movement. At first you enter a dream world in which skylarks sing and sheep bleat, as time stands still, but suddenly the world is full of wings and you wonder what's going on. Would I stand the test?

My traditional, stone-walled, horseshoe-shaped butt was a joy to behold, a credit to craftsmanship, and even contained a drain in the corner so that my feet should remain dry – a special problem with sunken or semi-sunk butts. For the last few weeks the keepers here, and their colleagues all over the country, had been busily 'butting', spending many hours in repairing and maintaining these shooting stations. Some butts had been in position for over a century, for generally grouse are creatures of habit and the experienced keeper knows just where they like to fly in relation to the local terrain and prevailing winds. A few butts are so well established they actually appear on large-scale Ordnance Survey maps.

Nonetheless, you can still see the ruined rows of butts which have been wrongly positioned, and sometimes you will come across more unsightly ones – usually of wood – which are of an experimental nature. Good as any shoot is, it should never stop searching for improvement. If the temporary butts are successful they may be replaced by permanent ones when funds permit. And occasionally a dry-stone wall which is already there serves perfectly well for the whole line.

The precise positioning of each butt must take into consideration many factors. Most are about 40–50m (44–55yd) apart so that any grouse coming through must be comfortably within range of at least one of the Guns (that is assuming the flankers dissuade the birds from bursting out the sides of the drives). On flat, open moors the butts must be placed in gills or valleys so that the shooting party may get in position without flushing the birds, but there is far greater flexibility on more undulating ground. In more open situations the butts should be sunken as the grouse will not fly over man so readily as the pheasant will.

The turves which are placed on the tops of the butts take a lot of punishment from the elements and sheep jump up on them to eat the heather, grasses and berries that grow there. Thus they need constant attention, but replacement turves should not be cut nearby as that would soon spoil the appearance of the shoot. Some sportsmen have to pay graziers for the right to cut such turves. And in well-grazed areas turfed butts are often covered with fencing to protect them from stock.

Where possible butts should be sunken to avoid scaring the grouse

My first butt had been dug so that my eye-level was just 60–90cm (2–3ft) above the surrounding ground, making any approaching grouse, skimming over the heather a more challenging target. It was one of a row of ten on a moor which had several rows on most of the drives, to cater for varying wind conditions. On this first drive, my loader told me, I would probably be a little out of the main action as the prevailing wind pushed the main flight of birds towards the other end of the line.

Eventually all was ready and it was warm enough for me to dispense with my topcoat, to allow greater freedom of movement. Loader Bill stood slightly behind me to my right, with number 2 gun at the ready and two further cartridges held firmly between his fingers so that he could take my first gun without dropping them. On his side hung a gannochy, containing further exposed cartridges for rapid loading, and very sensibly he sported a pair of ear muffs for there is no doubt that 'gun deafness' comes quickest to butt-shooters. A loader or companion is particularly vulnerable to this insidious malady as shots are often fired directly over his head. That said, I must confess that I rarely wear muffs or even plugs when I am game-shooting as I like to enjoy all the sounds of the countryside as well as pick up audible clues from approaching birds. In this case I savoured the relaxing sound of the bubbling brook behind me and tried to home in on snatches of conversation which drifted across from my more vociferous neighbours. Were they talking about me?

Then the headkeeper used his walkie-talkie to instruct the beaters to commence, the early team having already gathered birds from adjoining ground. How invaluable these little radios are. In the old days one of the outer flankers would have had to signal the start to a man or two posted specially to receive instructions. In addition, they allow organisers to fine-tune drives as they progress. Firing shots to start drives is a rather hit-or-miss affair where hills intervene and some of the men are slightly deaf. This can also unsettle the grouse.

Inevitably, the whole line suddenly realised that our concentration had been too much in one place as a whole covey swept over our heads unsaluted. But there was no way the next lot would catch me out.

The wait seemed endless. Would they ever come? And foolishly I rested my gun on the butt top, not realising quite how quick the grouse-shooter has to be. Bill looked fidgety and, on seeing what I'd done, tactfully remarked: 'I think they'll be coming now sir.' I took the hint and stood at the ready. Suddenly a big blue hare came lolloping over the horizon, progressing steadily, but unrushed like a long-distance runner. As soon as he saw me he froze and stretched up to assess the situation. Like a wise old man, he seemed to know that the beaters would be upon him soon and immediately determined that the only way out was sideways. Later we saw many hares, some of which bounded between the butts: they provided an unexpected spectacle for someone not used to the grouse-moor's rich diversity of wildlife.

Then Bill whispered: 'To your left sir,' and I spun round to investigate. I couldn't see a thing. 'Where? What?' I asked anxiously. 'Two birds,' replied Bill, 'but don't fret, they're away over Mr Campbell.' Unfortunately Mac didn't see them either and

Loaders are often keepers from neighbouring estates

we began to wonder what the organisers must have thought of us. Now I was even more determined.

Almost immediately came a volley of shots from over the rise, and infuriatingly I couldn't see what was going on. No time to dwell on it though for there, in the distance, were two specks which hugged the contours of the land, repeatedly disappearing against the dark background, and they were coming my way. This surely was it. But had they chosen me because I was the weakest link in the chain? Yes! Suddenly the specks were cannonballs and as they passed overhead they split like two of the Red Arrows and I missed a mile behind after dallying too long on target selection. After all the good advice and special lessons I'd failed. Once again I learned that there is no substitute for actual experience.

Immediately a larger bird hove into view and instinctively I brought the gun to double readiness, but the ever-diplomatic Bill quickly remarked: 'Oh look, a hen harrier,' obviously not wanting to risk his charge shooting a protected species. 'Yes,' I replied, 'they are splendid birds,' trying to make out that I was thoroughly familiar with them and that there was no way I would bag one in error.

Then a good covey appeared and, disappointingly for me, chose to pass several butts down. I was fascinated to see the puffs of gunsmoke whisked away on the gusty air and two birds fall in front before the sound of the shots reached me. And to my surprise there were two further puffs of smoke and two more tumbling bodies as the grouse powered away behind. 'Wow, some shooting,' I murmured to Bill, 'Aye,' he said slowly with an air of inevitability, 'that'll be Mr Parker – he's a very fine Shot.' I wondered if I would ever reach that standard.

Now came my chance to prove that I had fired a gun before: five birds chasing the wind at just the right height, though apparently set on visiting the next county. Bill crouched, I crouched and even the dog seemed to crouch as I felt the eyes of all Scotland bearing down on me. Remember what the man said, I told myself: 'bum, belly, beak, bang'. Bring the gun up smoothly through the bird and fire, never forgetting to follow through. So I did, and it worked, but I was only just on time as the covey turned on afterburners and there was no way I was up to a second shot. Instead, I shrank back into an insufferable pool of conceit, not saying anything and avoiding Bill's eyes, pretending that my new-found success was totally predictable. And as I savoured the triumph over long odds I quite forgot that I had to change guns, even though I'd fired only one barrel. Bill, of course, remained calm and, rather belatedly, but definitely without trace of surprise, said 'Nice shot sir' as he passed me number 2 gun.

So the battle was joined. Now I was a grouse-shooter and immediately set about achieving a whole string of ambitions. First I wanted to kill one well in front, then two in front, then two in front and one behind, and finally the ultimate accolade – two in front *and* two behind. Now my blood was truly up, but no sooner was I prepared for the next wave than the beaters topped the facing hill, their white, plastic flags waving rhythmically and cracking in the wind, and I was deflated because I knew that the drive would soon be over.

That was when I let my concentration slip again for I was totally unprepared for

The 'walkie-talkie' has become an essential part of drive control

the number of grouse which, one by one, rose from the last part of the drive. Is this one on? Is it safe? Is it my neighbour's? Questions, questions. Excuses, excuses. And just as I decided to give one a go the horn sounded for no more shooting in front. Fortunately, I must have had a rush of blood to the head, stayed calm, turned sweetly and downed this singleton behind as if I did it every day. And to heighten the arrogance I pulled it off in full view of all the beaters and keepers closing in on us. Now they would think I was one of the boys, an old hand who no bird could pass. Sadly, Bill knew better and at lunch he was sure to spill the beans.

Suddenly the hitherto empty moor was full of people and dogs, every one of whom, except me, appeared to know exactly what to do, yet nobody seemed to be giving any orders. Quietly, and without any fuss, they all systematically worked the entire area around the butts. 'Anything here?' asked a head-scarved lady who turned out to be one of several paid pickers-up. 'No thanks, just the two down and we've already got those,' I replied smugly, turning to admire my first brace, beautifully laid out atop the butt.

BURBERRY
COMPLETE SHOOTING KIT

The most comfortable and protective outrig for the moors. Designed by sportsmen for sportsmen, it assists skill by ensuring absolute freedom, keeps the wearer dry when it rains, warm when it is chilly, yet, naturally ventilating, is delightfully cool on the hottest day. The Kit consists of a

BURBERRY SUIT

—Jacket with Pivot Sleeves, as illustrated, or choice of twenty other workmanlike models, and Plus-Fours or Knicker-Breeches—in exclusive Burberry-proofed materials—Burberry Gabardine, Gamefeather, Silvering, Plus-Beau or Floretta Tweeds; and

THE BURBERRY

The ONE Weatherproof in which it is possible to shoot as quickly and accurately as when not wearing an Overcoat. Featherlight, thin and flexible, The Burberry makes no difference to the "set" of the gun and enables the sportsman to maintain top form healthfully protected against rain, mist or cold.

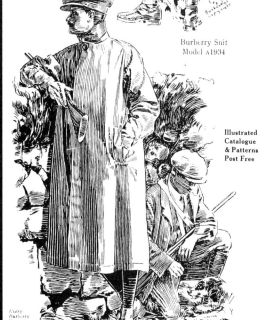

Burberry Suit
Model A1934

**Illustrated
Catalogue
& Patterns
Post Free**

*Every
Burberry
Garment
bears the
Burberry
Trade Mark*

The Burberry

BURBERRYS HAYMARKET
S.W.1 LONDON
8 & 10 BD. MALESHERBES PARIS ; & PROVINCIAL AGENTS
Burberrys Ltd.

*Burberrys
advertisement (1924)*

'Didn't you wing that first bird?' asked one of the keepers encouragingly. And for some odd reason I was tempted to say yes to save face, especially as Bill had moved away. But I remained honest: no way did I want to be branded as one of those selfish fools who never admits to missing and is always sending someone on a wild-goose chase.

Now the moor was a riot of colour as yellow labradors, black labradors, black-and-white springers, liver-and-white springers, setters and even a golden retriever plunged eagerly into the purple heather, coaxed by proud masters. Then there were the beaters – a real chocolate box of old and young, male and female, smart and scruffy, bright and dull. One slip of a schoolgirl was encased in yellow oilskin for all eventualities, while her brawny friend was quite warm enough in an Omo-white, short-sleeved shirt which stood out as well as his flag. Some were students on vacation, others looked pretty desperate for the tenner or so they would earn that day. And then there was old Squinty Jones – an unshaven sixty-four year old who lived nearby and had been beating on this one estate since he was fourteen. No wonder his skin resembled leather, but just why he could afford only string to keep his trousers up and a grubby old long-coat that a tramp would refuse I could not imagine. One thing was certain though – he was as fit as those youngsters. He had to be to walk 10 or 15 miles in those conditions on one day. Much luckier are the beaters on a moor owned by an Arab sheikh. They get £25 each even if he does not turn up. Sometimes he arrives at two or three in the afternoon, does three or four drives and goes home at 8pm!

As we walked back to the vehicles I reflected on my performance. The moor can be inspirational, the weather perfect, birds abundant, companions fun, and organisation excellent, but the Gun will never go home very happy if he feels that his marksmanship has been wanting. Yet, sadly, this is all too often the case in these increasingly commercial days when wealthy Guns can buy fine sport which is, certainly at first, way beyond their natural capabilities. They simply have not been brought up to shoot fluently and, when accumulated wealth allows them to come to the sport in later life, most of them are just that bit too slow for the King of Gamebirds.

Some people say that this does not matter, that the estates need the money and the sport should go to those who can best afford it. But try telling that to the dedicated teams who have produced such fine entertainment. You can see the disappointment in their faces when hopelessly inexperienced Guns miss bird after bird and show no inkling of gradual improvement. Of course, big tips from these *nouveau* gunners make the pill less bitter, but it can never buy sporting esteem. Fortunately, it appeared that our team was doing quite well overall because we had all had proper schooling in gunnery, beginning with mixed bags on rough-shoots and progressing to the finest driven pheasants before even coming to the moor. A guest who had never held a gun before, let alone had a shooting lesson, would almost certainly be totally demoralised on a good driven grouse-shoot.

As we reassembled, one of the Americans on his first visit said to me 'Boy, are they fast!' Then, as we parted, a loader who overheard him whispered: 'He should be here in October – he won't even see them.' Apart from the likelihood of ever-wilder weather as autumn progresses, grouse are undoubtedly much more intelligent than hand-reared pheasants, or even wild partridges, and readily use their keen eyesight and marvellous manoeuvrability to outwit both beaters and Guns. Modern grouse-shooters often overlook the importance of adequate concealment. For example, a man is expected to fit into a butt regardless of how tall he is, whereas in the old days it was common to have extra turves to hand so that each sportsman could adjust the butt height.

Butts should never be placed on the skyline or anywhere near it because the grouse will spot them and anybody moving in them at great distances. This is a rare mistake nowadays, though it is not that unusual to see butts which are below, but too near, the skyline so that even the best of shooters have insufficient notice of a bird's approach. A hollow in which the Guns can see birds approaching from either side is ideal, but you have to remember that some moors are very restricted in their terrain.

It was such a little hollow that provided the setting for our second drive, and I was pleased because I had always considered myself to be fairly good at snap-shooting. There was no question at all that I would have to be at battle stations throughout this drive and it was essential to lock on to any target the moment it hit the skyline, for then it was already in range. Unless I was incredibly lucky, I could forget two birds in front there. On other drives, where there was more notice of oncomers, I was advised to mark a patch of heather way out in front as the spot where the first target must not be allowed to pass. About halfway between there and the butt would be the ideal place to bag number two. Assuming a covey approached at moderate height, the first bird would be taken just at the point when no forward allowance, or lead, is necessary, but that is not to say that the Gun's swing should be stopped abruptly.

When it comes to the gun itself, then I would advise the steadiness of a side-by-side for grouse – in practice you will rarely see an over-and-under on a decent grouse-shoot. Twelve-bore is standard, lighter guns not really being up to the job any more than light loads and small shot are (5 and 6 are ideal). Don't forget that a hurtling grouse can take some stopping. A relatively short gun suits most Shots, because it is easier to handle in the butt situation, but, when you get down towards the legal limit of 24in, barrel flip may become a problem. The degree of choke is not that important providing that it is fairly open – no more than a quarter – and, when coupled with the chosen load, inspires the user's confidence in taking on birds at all possible ranges. Both barrels should be bored the same to achieve consistency and it is best to stick to the same make of cartridge, once a good, consistent performer has been found. All this I had the benefit of.

As we waited, Bill explained how the keepers there had burnt patches of heather both in front and behind the butts to stop grouse gathering in front of the Guns and to make the subsequent pick-up easier. He also pointed out that this time the grouse would be driven into the wind – something not generally possible with partridges and requiring a skilled team of beaters and flankers.

Flanking is not just a question of arbitrary flag-waving, as we see all too often. Whether on the grouse-moor or partridge manor, the flanker can make or break a drive. He should not be merely a man who can no longer stand the pace of a full day's beating or one who is getting deaf, but one who is experienced, trustworthy and can

Shooting at Gunnerside. Ear protection is a sensible precaution against 'gun deafness'

work quickly on his own initiative. His flag should not be waving all the time but only as necessary to turn birds not going in the required direction. The element of surprise is very important and the flanker must be prepared to run to a new position as necessary, provided that it is safe to do so. Unnecessary flag-waving may turn birds which are already coming in well to the butts. Sometimes back-flankers are stationed behind the butts to help turn birds towards the next drive. The main flankers are stationed to the sides of the beating line, which is like a giant horseshoe and becomes increasingly shallow as it advances towards the butts.

Although I could not see the beaters on our second drive I knew there were only about a dozen, widely spread. With such a thin line early in the season most of the young birds are not flushed but nearly all the old birds come forward, which is a good way to get rid of these undesirables. But when that part of the moor is driven, say a month later, a much larger team is necessary to move the stronger, more experienced young as well as old birds. Sometimes the headkeeper, or keeper in charge of the line, carries a flag of a distinctive colour with which he can signal the flankers. His role is especially important on undulating ground, where you can never be sure which part of the advancing line a grouse will see first. On flat ground it is relatively easy to move the birds smoothly towards the butts, but should hillocks intervene and one side of the beating line show itself first then the grouse are likely to speed off in the wrong direction. This is where the well-positioned keeper can signal a flanker to intervene. That flanker must keep low and spring to action at the critical moment so that the startled birds are turned over the Guns before they know what is happening. And in the interests of safety it is most important that the shooters are made aware of the flankers' positions, some of which may be between beaters and butts.

It was intriguing to think of all these skilful manoeuvres taking place out of sight while I waited in my butt, wondering just how many Guns never even bother to find out what goes on behind the scenes. To my left, my friend Dick was practising his

The loader will often spot approaching grouse before the Gun does

swing, and to my right the next butt was out of sight, but a thoughtfully placed marker stick indicated its position. Thus, although I could not possibly have scored a direct hit on my concealed neighbour, I was reminded of the perils of dropping shot, not to mention the risk of shooting his birds.

Suddenly four dark shapes appeared like a squadron of Harriers over the ridge before me. I slipped off the safety as the gun rose like a magnet to my shoulder, and the two leading birds cartwheeled into the heather while those flying point split down the line, denying me the chance of a going-away double. A puff of feathers dispersed on the August breeze and a spattering of shots suggested that the survivors' luck was continuing. Bill handed me number 2 gun and I settled to readdress the action, reflecting on the way those very stiff-winged birds had collapsed like jelly at my right-and-left, their tremendous speed carrying them a remarkable distance before they hit the heather. I knew what it was like to be hit by a dead pheasant and had no wish to catch a far-faster grouse on my hooter.

After this splendid drive, during which I felt like one receiving serve from the Wimbledon champion, we reassembled at the vehicles for a much-welcome noggin.

Guest Guns take lunch on Byrecleugh Moor

There was soup and sherry, sloe gin and cans of Tartan bitter, the latter a great favourite with the Americans. At this point we were joined by the Duke, who took great interest in every detail and went into lengthy discussions with the headkeeper after picking a few birds with his young labrador. And as we relaxed, comparing notes and savouring the upland environment, the keepers started to separate the old and young birds, which were then carefully placed into wooden crates.

After one more drive, we drove to a purpose-built lunch hut, wonderfully situated high on the moor. It was a modern building with a magnificent view over the hillside and I felt rather guilty sitting in it, enjoying salmon, lobster and fine wines while the keepers and beaters either sat on the damp ground or in their vehicles munching great doorsteps of sandwiches. I much prefer those shoots where the employees too can enjoy their well-earned break under cover – if necessary in a separate building. Some moors still have the little stone or brick buildings in which Guns sheltered over a century ago. These blend so well with the wild moorlands.

Outside I could hear the headkeeper, a forbidding man who had been enticed away from his native Yorkshire, giving orders for the afternoon: 'Right you lads – I want you flankin' ont' top butts.' Inside we were joined by the wives of the Americans and some of the Duke's family, so the small-talk ranged beyond the shooting field. Helping to serve was the headkeeper's daughter, but why she and some of her friends were not at school I cannot imagine. I asked her if she ever got fed up with looking after a whole covey of giggling strangers like us. 'There's no way I'm staying at home,' she replied. 'I'll have a grand feast when you're all gone.' But inevitably, as it was the Glorious Twelfth, there was discussion of neighbouring shoots and the traditional friendly rivalry: 'I hear High Button's been badly hit by disease this year . . . Bloody rent-a-mob antis due at Colonel Trotter's today . . . You mean you haven't been to Kipling Hill? . . . That was a great shot of yours on the last drive Tom . . . Keep that up and we ought to beat Lord J's lot today.'

But just as we were sinking into that blissful state of relaxation known only to the fieldsportsman, the headkeeper loomed dark in the doorway and strode over to our host to whisper something into his ear. Immediately, the sporting agent leapt to his feet and announced that unless we were all on parade in two minutes the next drive would be cancelled. Spoil-sport? Of course not: in my experience such gatherings of 'high-achievers' love the novelty of being bullied, and there are always one or two dull individuals who would shoot all day without interruption, given free rein. And yet such selfishness is counter-productive because a team without rest – especially the keepers and beaters – becomes jaded and loses interest, merely going through the motions. A few shoots do prefer to shoot right through lunch and end the day with a slap-up supper, at which alcohol may be taken without fear of tiredness and lack of attention to safety. However, if this is the case then there must be at least enough beaters to allow staggered breaks.

Our relief lasted the customary hour or so, most other shoots varying their allowance between three-quarters of an hour and an unusually generous one and a half hours.

Ed Littlefield is a skilled bagpipes player. Here he entertains at Byrecleugh

Keeping an eye on the birds while changing guns

But not all sustain themselves on luxury fodder such as salmon and champagne, as we had done. In fact, it is the commercial shoots which seem to major in luxury, whereas more wholesome and sustaining food such as steak and kidney pie or oxtail is more likely to be forthcoming on private days, for richer Guns find little novelty in feasting. One disadvantage in putting on a veritable banquet is that the Guns are generally denied the opportunity of picnicking in the open, surrounded by bulging hampers and wild, beckoning horizons. A nice compromise is to put tables outside, but suitably warm days become harder to find as the season progresses. On this occasion we had no choice.

With the unequalled taste of vintage port still fresh on my tongue, it was a bit of a shock to find myself thrust back into a butt, the stub of an American cigar still glowing between my fingers and a freshening wind searching out the chinks in my armour. This was to be the day's longest drive, but there was plenty of entertainment as Bill, who had also enjoyed a tongue-loosener or two, gave me the low-down on the boss, the boss's wife, the factor, and all the Guns who had ever fired a shot within 50 miles.

A grouse retrieved. Good dogs can increase the pick-up by 10 per cent or more

I was glad that I bothered to pack my waterproofs because the very first cloud that came over seemed determined to discharge its entire contents on our little hill, as did all the others which followed it with increasing frequency as the day wore on. And at the same time we appreciated that the grouse-shooter's hat is no mere sop to fashion. Gloves, too, are useful in such conditions, when slipping the safety catch may not be easy with cold, wet hands.

The order of the drives had been carefully worked out according to whether they generally do best in the morning or the afternoon, the wind and weather, and the expediency of moving birds into position for the next exercise. However, our weather forecast was not too accurate and it was then that the headkeeper's generalship came to notice. His experience had taught him to 'follow the birds', so, after the customary consultation with the boss, a change of plan was announced. How important it is to have a man with such initiative. Such changes are not taken lightly because grouse take much longer than partridges – up to about six hours according to the density of the population – to return home, and any mistake may result in insufficient birds for subsequent drives.

We were not to be disappointed. The birds seemed to take the wind to their hearts and came at us like Stookers, with surprising verve for the first day of the season. Never had it been so important to select birds without hesitation, and even then there was often the need to supplement the smooth swing with that instinctive flick on to secure sufficient lead in the split second before pulling the trigger. It is a peculiar thing which only experience can teach. But even when you are conscious of doing this the movement of the gun must be continued after firing so that when the shot leaves the muzzle the required lead is maintained. Although most people can never see a shot string, it is not that fast, so bringing the gun to an abrupt halt on squeezing the trigger will result in miss after miss and a dull day all round. Also, as you discharge the first barrel you should be aware of your next target. Do not hang around watching what happens to the first bird: with experience you will know the outcome as soon as you pull the trigger. Indeed, it seems as if you are unable to pull out of a certain miss when your trigger finger is committed. And always remember that with double guns your ambition is to shoot two birds in front and two behind. Do not expect anyone else to tell you how much time you will need. Only you can sort out the complex reactions of your senses.

The remaining two drives of my first Twelfth just flashed past as I really got into my stride and started to enjoy every minute. Indeed, it was a very carefully constructed day which ended on a high note and made sure that we all wanted to come again. The birds had come steadily and everyone had their fair share of sport. I'll never forget the face of Tony Francesco from California, when he emerged from a butt with his first-ever brace of grouse. As he held them aloft his grin was as wide as the Atlantic which had hitherto divided us.

When we piled back into the misted-up vehicles a sudden quiet came over us as we reflected on such a scintillating experience. Briefly, each man was alone in his little world of blurred impressions, reliving the triumphs and missed opportunities, still pumped full of adrenalin, yet physically tired and glad to sit down. Then, as if

Above: *Paying the pickers-up*   Below: *Regrouping after a successful drive*

at some unseen signal, everyone started to babble. 'Helluva day guys' . . . 'Thank God I had a spare pair of eyes loading for me' . . . 'Is there a John on board?' . . . 'Can we eat these birds tonight?' . . . 'Wait till I tell Inky about this place' . . . 'Put me down for next year' . . . 'Pity all the bloody grouse are in the north'. I leave you to sort out which were the American comments.

Back at the shooting lodge, the keepers unloaded the rest of the birds and laid out the entire bag in neat rows on the grass verge. Rather more than we dared hope for given the relative inexperience of the majority of Guns: '107 brace', announced the headkeeper, and everyone felt deep satisfaction in a job well done.

Various people whizzed off so quickly you would think we had only ten minutes to live, but most hung around, peering at the birds, marvelling at the plumage, expressing curiosity at this and that – 'How did that hare get in the bag?' – and enjoying a dram from a generous hip-flask. The headkeeper took great pains to select a brace of birds for me to take home (at £500 each I should savour every mouthful) and I slipped him a couple of tenners for his trouble, as I did my loader. The various groups who had been temporarily thrown together in sporting brotherhood bid fond farewells and we all sped off to our homes and hotels for a soak in the tub before rallying to relive the entire day over a very long dinner.

Beva advertisement (1928)

11

Walking Tall

Walking-up and dogging for grouse are much cheaper than driving,
but for many purists provide far richer sport

When driving game became fashionable in the mid-nineteenth century it was inevitable that it attracted criticism from traditionalists. As we saw in Chapter 4, one of the most outspoken was the remarkable Lewis Clement, who was to found the *Shooting Times*. He considered the new system in relation to grouse-shooting in his 1877 book *Shooting, Yachting and Sea-fishing Trips*. He admitted that 'owing to the wily nature of grouse, driving must occasionally be resorted to in order to bag them' but 'that driving should be enthusiastically denominated "the sport *par excellence*" must be simply a joke.'

For Clement the essentials of sport had to include 'seeking game on its own ground, and, in so doing, giving it free scope to use its wits for eluding our approach.' Then, 'when we have succeeded in getting within range, we must be clever enough to kill our game in whatever manner and direction it chooses to try to escape our guns.' He maintained that in driving

> . . . the first of these conditions is entirely discarded, and the second is only partly fulfilled, inasmuch as speed alone, and that in one direction only, ie towards the shooters, is sought to be allowed to the birds as a means of escape, therefore driving cannot be classed as sportsmanlike.

But, of course, he exaggerated the situation to suit his argument for there can be immense variety in the way grouse approach the butts.

'To succeed in reaching game on its own ground,' he continued, 'requires the sportsman a personal knowledge of the haunts and habits of his game. Now the driver of our day need not know where his grouse live, neither does he need to know their habits, their tricks, and how to thwart them. The birds' wiles are driven away by the irresistible *cordon* of beaters.' Thus, said Clement, a driven grouse-shooter may be a good Shot but he 'cannot be called a sportsman'. For him the only real sport in grouse-shooting was 'the very difficulty one experiences in getting within range of the wary birds.'

Then there was the excuse that some landowners could only spare a few days on which to shoot their grouse. But, said Clement, 'that is no reason why those who live on their estates should imitate them and kill everything in the first week.' Others protested that driving was the only way to eliminate old birds, and Clement agreed, but, he pointed out, the young were also shot indiscriminately for it would take a pretty sharp man to tell them apart on the wing.

Another defence of driving was that 'the more birds they kill the more are found in the next season', to which Clement remarked: 'If that is the case, why, after every successful drive, are the moors restocked from live grouse bought from poachers in other counties.' Now here Clement may be excused for not being aware of the relationship between grouse population density and shooting through culling diseased birds, but I cannot believe that the transportation of live grouse was significant.

Quite rightly, he attributed all the 'generalship' in driving to the headkeeper, for he alone is responsible for gathering and presenting the birds, but today more owners share the decisions. Most Guns remain ignorant of how the grouse get in front of them.

Clement also conceded that driven grouse are generally harder to hit because they are much faster than the average going-away bird which has just been put up. But as to the system, 'I cannot bring my mind to consider it fair in any way whatsoever . . . hiding behind a battery and firing from behind a mantlet at an unsuspecting bird.'

Then there was the question of gathering wounded birds quickly, and the 'cruelty' of grouse-drivers in 'allowing wretched birds to die a lingering death, exposed to the ardent rays of the sun, or with a downpour of rain and sleet falling upon their mangled bodies for hours together before they are picked up, and their sufferings put to an end.' Shooting slowly, over dogs, he argued, enabled every wounded grouse to be captured and despatched rapidly. However, you have to remember that he lived in very different times, when many driven-game shooters were primarily after big bags to boost their ego and nothing was allowed to slow them down. Today, however, the scene is very different as bags are much smaller. Well-positioned teams of pickers-up immediately gather wounded birds which fall well behind the Guns, while other dogs, including the Guns' own, are generally on hand to retrieve wounded birds near the butts. Admittedly there will be wounded birds in front which, in the interests of safety, may not be retrieved for some minutes, but their numbers are relatively small and today every effort is made to collect them quickly, by incoming flankers and beaters as well as Guns and pickers-up.

Then there was the immense difference in numbers of shots fired.

A sportsman who in the open, over Don and Ponto, shoots ten birds with a dozen barrels is far more clever than the 'driver' who kills 500 grouse in a thousand shots or more from behind a wall. There the distinction remains – one is a sportsman, the other is simply a shooter, more or less skilled.

Clement was also concerned about the very large amount of game which occasionally came on to the market as a result of driving.

Such enormous quantities of grouse make their simultaneous appearance in the market that it gets quite glutted, and even the very poor may then eat grouse. As far as the public is concerned this is but a cause for congratulation; but the game-preservers must make a very wry face over it when a consignment of game fetches say but £30 or £40, instead of £250.

The Queen Mother at Balmoral Gundog Trial

Today this is not much of a problem because the grouse is such a popular table bird its price remains generally high. But with pheasants there have been major problems in recent years: the sport has become so popular the *national* bag of *predominantly reared* birds has increased tremendously even though individual bags have generally diminished. Unfortunately, the modern British public is not that keen on game and few people are prepared to experiment because the advantages of a glut rarely seem to be reflected in lower shop prices.

In the old walk-up days much of the grouse-shooting was undertaken by the gamekeepers, who went out frequently to shoot a few birds for their masters' dining-tables. It was quite a while before most of the landowners realised what fun their men were having in performing this 'chore' and decided to have a go themselves. For a relatively short time the gentlemen gunners became the true hunters who Clement admired.

But Lew had no time for the big Shots who adopted driving.

Some shooters have been looked upon by admiring writers as models of strength, perseverance, skill and endurance, for not having got their fingers or shoulders hurt, and for standing the explosions of so many hundreds of shots without being driven crazy by the noise! That the shooters' fingers did not get abrased only proves that the fowling-pieces they used were good guns, whose triggers did not shake as some Brummagen concerns would have done. That their shoulders did not get sore proves that the guns were no kickers, or that they were properly loaded, or both; for all that sort of thing, the shooters deserve not the slightest credit. And as for the brain nerve that can endure the 'din' of so many shots, I sincerely congratulate, not the shooters, but their attendants, who proved that they could stand it without going mad.

The sportsman, being intent on 'watching his game fall or escape, is perfectly unconscious of the din.'

Notwithstanding Clement's grousing, grouse-driving is a glorious sport and it attracts many thousands of people who would have neither the time nor inclination to walk-up. Others would be too frail or unfit. Could there be just a few 'sour grapes' among those who cannot afford the dearer activity? The truth is that both driving and walking are excellent and *different* activities, the comparison of which is futile. There are plenty of men (and a scattering of women) who enjoy both: surely they are the real sportsmen.

Walking-up

Just what is this walking-up, 'original-hunter' idea now vigorously defended to the point of snobbishness?, mere 'butt-buffs' being regarded as effete. Well, to put it simply, it is a form of rough-shooting, but because the habitat – the heather moor – is more or less uniform, special techniques have evolved, and because that habitat is hilly and difficult to walk over the participants must be very fit indeed.

Some people are primarily interested in the dog work involved, and that is fine,

A well-trained labrador must also be thoroughly fit for picking-up in heather

but when they take it to such extremes that the shooting becomes almost superfluous, then they too might be accused of not being 'true hunters'. They might as well confine themselves to field trials, just as the big-bag boys should turn their attention to clay-pigeon shooting. Perhaps the person who derives the maximum pleasure in the field is the one who delights in many things. He wants to find and outwit the quarry himself, but regards his dogs as no more than useful 'tools' in this work because he is equally concerned with enjoying the exercise, the wide-ranging wildlife about him, and the spectacular moorland environment in all its many moods. At the same time he is interested in results, at least a few birds in the bag. And contrary to what some people say, *no one* carries on shooting for very long without something to show for his trouble, no matter how much he enjoys the sight of the peregrine passing or the low, winter sun dipping over the horizon.

Dogging for grouse, with specialist breeds in the way of our grandfathers, should not be confused with mere walking-up, which does not necessarily include dogs at all. Simple walking-up involves a small team of Guns – say six – tramping across a moor in line, along a chosen route, shooting those grouse which happen to rise. This does not demand the use of so-called 'bird-dogs', though the Guns should be accompanied by competent retrievers, labradors being preferred to spaniels because the shorter-legged dogs will tire more rapidly during a long day in the heather, and their longer coats are a hindrance in hot weather.

Walking-up has become extremely popular in recent years because it is generally very cheap, does not require a kennel of specialist dogs which are not needed for most of the year, and enables participants to enjoy the real countryside. It is a wonderful pursuit for a group of chums on an economy holiday, but it is essential that, while everyone may not be an Olympic athlete, the whole team are of similar fitness. If there is a weak link in the chain it will spoil everyone's fun, as will the tireless bore determined to bolster his macho image.

One of the great things about walking-up is that you are free of the worries of interconnecting drives, but that is not to say that some thought should not be given to the starting and finishing points. The advice of the keeper should be sought and a circuitous route worked out so that the best chances may be taken and fresh ground taken in all day. It is surprisingly easy to get lost on relatively featureless moorland so the team must be accompanied by someone who knows the ground well. Guns should ensure that they do not wander too far apart and always keep each other in sight. If two Guns part company to walk either side of a steep hilltop or other obstacle they may find they have lost contact on emerging at the other side. When this happens it is essential to get back together immediately as the smallest mistake can become a major problem if the lost individual goes boring on alone. It is a good idea to have a prearranged signal to stop and start the line after a bird has been shot and gathered.

Walking often involves tramping across a surprisingly wide variety of habitat, so be prepared. One moment the heather will be short, dry and springy and you will be bounding along on top of the world. Suddenly, it will became lank and apparently neglected where it has not been burnt in recent years, and it will conceal pot-holes and bogs into which you will inevitably tumble, no matter how careful you are. If you do fall it is almost certain to happen just when your first or only chance of a shot comes along. But whatever you do, do not languish there sulking like a baby because it is unlikely that any of the others will be aware of your predicament and you will soon be left behind. At first you will curse and mutter to yourself: 'Why do they walk so fast, why are all the traps in my path and why are they so much fitter than me?' But then, just as you wish you were back at home, someone will call halt and you will have the chance to recuperate and compare notes. You can lean back on the mattress of heather, enjoy a squashed sandwich from your pocket and let the red in your cheeks subside.

Do not be tempted to sit for too long or eat and drink too much or else you may suffer severe stiffness, cramps and wind when you start up again. The rolling hills will draw you ever onwards, beyond every horizon there is another, probably more mountainous, and just to keep you on your toes the most precipitous slopes will be sprinkled with loose scree. Yet despite all the hardships you must remain absolutely alert at all times because without bird-dogs to mark for you the shots will always come when you least expect them.

Lady Biddulph enjoys a little lobster for lunch, on the outstanding grouse moor built up by her late husband

Some of the helpers take lunch at Byrecleugh

Hold your gun firmly with both hands, at the ready at all times, and always pointing forward where it cannot endanger those at either side of you. Do not slip the safety catch until bringing the gun up to shoot, and if more than one bird rises be positive in your target selection. Although walked-up birds are usually easier to shoot than driven ones they will become noticeably trickier as the season progresses and adept at using even the lightest wind to jink away sideways and spoil your aim. Do not be surprised if, at the end of the day, you return home with little more than proof that you really are still young and fit enough to keep up with the boys. But do be astonished if you have not acquired an insatiable appetite for a great sport.

Dogging for Grouse

Shooting with bird-dogs is a different thing altogether, requiring much more cunning and patience than straightforward walking-up. And notice that I have not used the

The beaters approach, flags flapping in the wind, and the end of the drive is nigh

common expression 'over bird-dogs' because, taken literally, that is a bad thing, as we shall see.

In dogging, a small team of Guns – ideally two and certainly not more than four – walk the moor and shoot grouse which are located by a variety of specialist dogs with amazing scenting ability. The dogs are under the close control of their handlers at all times, leaving the Guns free to concentrate on their shooting. Other than that, a lad or two to carry the shot game is useful, as is a second team of dogs held well back, so that they may be rested and worked alternately.

In the old days most large estates had their own teams of grouse-dogs, but today few find this an economic proposition and only a few real enthusiasts continue the tradition. Neither is it still common for teams of dogs to be hired out and handled by resident estate keepers. However, some field triallers welcome the opportunity to work their dogs for shooting parties and may well be happy to oblige as long as their expenses are covered. Others are in great demand and rightly receive reasonable fees.

Anyone contemplating buying his own grouse-dogs – at least three are necessary for a busy programme – should be prepared to pay several hundred pounds each for reasonable, trained animals and up to about £150 each for puppies from a reliable source. Choosing the latter may be a costly mistake if they are put in the hands of a keeper devoid of dog-sense. But once this initial outlay has been made it can be cheaper to keep the dogs all year – especially as part of a larger kennel – than hire animals of the same quality and experience, especially with handlers. In addition, resident dogs are useful for spring counting of grouse pairs and for assessing shooting prospects later on.

Even if the animals are not required for any other form of hunting, there is a confusing choice of bird-dog and in the end some people are guided by little more than fancy or fashion. Pointers and setters were the elegant hounds featured in most of the old shooting pictures, and they certainly remain the most popular bird-dogs today. But irrespective of breed, all grouse-dogs should be well broken and very fit before the season commences.

Dogging is especially worthwhile in those parts where the grouse are thin on the ground or continually lie close so that driving is not worthwhile, places such as Caithness and Sutherland on the northern Scottish mainland and in the Western Isles. And the sparser the grouse population the greater the call for setters, which generally range wider than pointers, are less tender-footed and generally hardier. Pointers are particularly prone to sore feet at the beginning of the season. In the old days they used to try to harden the pads through soaking them in strong brine at the end of the day. But setters have their problems too. Irish are often relatively difficult to train and handle and English seem to have been down in quality and numbers of late. Perhaps Gordons are the most adaptable and successful at present.

Provided their feet are hard and round, pointers remain the first choice of many bird-doggers. They are chiefly guided by that magnificent head, the 'knowledge box', which ought to be broad between the ears, which should hang down close, with a fall

Burberrys advertisement (1922)

"Weather Prospects Unsettled"

Sportsmen Going North
should take
BURBERRY
WEATHERPROOF KIT

Then if it Rains, Blows or Swelters
Comfort and Security are Assured.

UNCERTAIN WEATHER

counts for little if the Shooting Kit be BURBERRY, because, made in closely-woven Burberry-proofed materials, it prevents the penetration of drizzle or downpour, and provides healthful warmth when there's a "nip" in the air. On the other hand

IF THE DAY BE FINE

Burberry is equally serviceable. The cloths, although weatherproof, are self-ventilating, airylight and cool—just the thing for tramping over rough country under a hot sun. Apart from protective powers

BURBERRY SUITS

actively assist skill. Pivot Sleeves and expanding pleats perfect arm and shoulder freedom, whilst practical design, accurate balance and ample pocket accommodation, each contribute to the comfort essential to the full enjoyment of moorland sport.

Illustrated
Catalogue
& Patterns
Post Free

Burberry Shooting Suits
can be supplied in all
sizes READY-TO-WEAR
or to order in 2 to 4 days

BURBERRY SHOOTING SUIT
MODEL A 1800

BURBERRY SHOOTING SUIT
MODEL A 1801

BURBERRY SHOOTING SUIT
MODEL A 1803

BURBERRY SHOOTING SUIT
MODEL A 1802

THE BURBERRY
For wet or cold days The Burberry is the ONE weatherproof in which it is possible to shoot as quickly and accurately as when not wearing an Overcoat.
Airylight and thin in texture, it makes no difference to the "set" of the gun and enables the sportsman to maintain top form, comfortably protected against drenching rain, mist or wind.

BURBERRYS HAYMARKET
S.W.1 LONDON
8 & 10 BD. MALESHERBES PARIS; & PROVINCIAL AGENTS
Burberrys Ltd.

The pickers-up at Bolton Abbey

or dent under the eyes. The nose should be long but not too broad, the nostrils very soft and moist. It is a dog which 'thinks' with its nose and is a magnificent athlete. But do not confuse the superior English pointer with the German shorthaired pointer because the latter is only any good when birds are thick on the ground. Whereas a pointer 'points' – standing upright with one paw raised – when it has winded game, a setter 'sets' by crouching. However, nowadays it is not the fashion for these breeds to retrieve the shot grouse: this is left to specialist retrievers such as labradors while the bird-dogs move on to find more quarry.

In this exacting sport careful observation of the wind is the first consideration, both at the start of the day and the beginning of every movement. Much will depend on the dogs' experience, and there is great fun to be had in watching them learn. Novices may point every living thing on the hill, from larks to moths, but they soon discover which scents are desirable and before too long the handler should be able to tell exactly what has been detected by his dog's posture and position. Not only will the dog's nuances of behaviour indicate the species located but also how far ahead the birds are, whether they are running or sitting tight, and perhaps even that he has found a covey rather than a single grouse.

Lady Biddulph takes a grouse from her young labrador

In the morning it is a good idea to start on the higher ground and work the grouse down to the lower feeding-grounds, with the evening providing the best sport. Early in the season the custom is to start at the downwind end of the beat and work across the wind, driving the grouse forward as far as possible, and turning into the wind whenever the beat boundary is reached. But when the wind is strong this could lead to birds turning back over the Guns and being lost for the day over the boundary. Then it is advisable to start upwind and work downwind, though still zigzagging. Working the ground well during the morning, so that the same birds are flushed several times, should ensure good sport in the afternoon because the broods are scattered and individual birds sit tighter, allowing closer approach.

When birds lie close later in the season it may be necessary to work directly downwind. Then, as the grouse are obliged to rise into the wind, they will give the

Guns a better chance if they get up wild. During the hot weather of August the young broods are most likely to be found about the sloping sides of burns and in mixed patches of heather and bracken. Then older birds tend to seek out rushy areas and rough grass, whose seeds they enjoy.

It is essential for Guns to remain silent throughout such exercises so a dog that requires vocal signals will be useless. The ground must always be worked thoroughly and the dogs not allowed to range too far from the Guns. Ideally, there will be one Gun each side, about 10–15m (12–16yd) from the dog and slightly ahead of it, the whole team moving in on the birds at the same speed. No shots should be fired directly over the head of the dog or so close as to endanger it. When a shot is taken the whereabouts of all dogs and companions must be known. Obviously those birds which rise on the left are targets for the left-hand Gun, just as those on the right belong to the man on the right. If a covey gets up more or less centrally then concentrate on those birds on your side. Always proceed with great care and patience: it is surprising how grouse may remain sitting tight nearby even after shots have been fired at other birds.

With the heather in full bloom on a sparkling August day this is a magnificent sport: no wonder it is enjoying a revival. Some estates have even brought back the old pannier ponies to complete the nostalgic picture, and just one or two have recently been out with muzzle-loaders to get some idea of how grandad used to do it. Most of us are quite happy with modern breechloaders though, especially as the fug created by grandad's black powder used to spoil the chance of a second shot. But one thing that remains the same for everyone is the wonderful opportunity to participate in a sport which never fails to relax frayed nerves and revive jaded spirits. The weather is almost always inspirational because dogging is far better in fair weather, with a warm, light breeze to waft the air scent. When it is wet the grouse move out into the open to avoid saturated cover but then they can see the shooting party more easily and do not allow close approach.

Incidentally, it is wrong to assume that good sportsmanship and relatively small bags have always been the hallmarks of dogging and walking-up grouse. On the contrary, in the days before driving became popular there were plenty of men vying to be top Gun and they concentrated more on maximising their killing than enjoying the simple delights of the moor. Indeed, the situation was serious enough to warrant stern comment from John Wilson (alias Christopher North) in the early nineteenth century:

We do not admire that shooting ground which resembles a poultry-yard. Grouse and barn-door fowls are constructed on opposite principles; the former being wild, the latter tame creatures, when in their respective perfection . . . Some shooters we know, sick of common sport, love slaughter. From sunrise to sunset of the first day of the moors they must bag their hundred brace. That can only be done when pouts prevail, and cheepers keep chiding, and where you have half a dozen attendants to head your double barrels *sans* intermission, for a round dozen of hours spent in perpetual fire. Commend us to a plentiful sprinkling of

NIGHT TRAINS TO SCOTLAND FOR THE TWELFTH

The finest fleet of trains in the world steams North to Scotland every day and is specially augmented for the 12th. Day and night they leave Euston, King's Cross and St. Pancras with their restaurants and sleeping-cars (first and third class) and their excellent staffs of servants. Below is a full list of night trains. Times of day trains will be supplied on request at any L M S or L·N·E·R station or office.

FROM EUSTON (L M S)
WEEKDAYS

P.M.
7.20 **AB** "The Royal Highlander"—Perth, Boat of Garten, Inverness, Aberdeen.

7.30 **AB** Oban.

7.40 **AB** Stirling, Gleneagles, Dundee.

8.0 **A** Dumfries, Stranraer Harbour, Turnberry.

9.25 Glasgow (On Saturdays, Third Class Sleeping Accommodation only).

10.50 Edinburgh, Stirling, Gleneagles, Perth, Dundee, Aberdeen, Inverness.

11.45 "Night Scot"—Glasgow.

A.M.
12.30 **DE** Dumfries, Kilmarnock, Glasgow.

SUNDAYS

P.M.
7.20 **B** "The Royal Highlander"—Perth, Boat of Garten, Inverness.

7.30 **B** Stirling, Oban, Gleneagles, Perth, Dundee, Aberdeen.

8.30 Dumfries, Stranraer, Turnberry.

9.30 Glasgow (Cent.).

10.50 Edinburgh, Stirling, Gleneagles, Perth, Dundee, Aberdeen, Oban.

11.45 "Night Scot"—Glasgow.

NOTES : **A** Saturdays excepted. **B** Dining Car Euston to Crewe.
D Saturday nights and Sunday mornings excepted. **E** Sleeping Cars to Kilmarnock.

FROM KING'S CROSS (L·N·E·R)
WEEKDAYS AND SUNDAYS

P.M.
*7.25 **R** "The Highlandman"—Edinburgh, Fort William (Breakfast car attached en route). Perth, Inverness.

*7.40 **R** "The Aberdonian"—Edinburgh, Dundee, Aberdeen, Elgin, Lossiemouth.

†10.25 "The Night Scotsman"—Glasgow. Dundee, Aberdeen, Perth.

P.M.
†10.35 Edinburgh, Glasgow. (North Berwick. First class only and on Friday nights only.)

A.M.
§1.5 After-Theatre Sleeping and Breakfast Car Train. Edinburgh, Glasgow, Dundee, Aberdeen, Perth, Inverness.

* Nightly (except Saturdays). † Nightly. § Daily (except Sunday mornings).
R Restaurant Car King's Cross to York.

FROM ST. PANCRAS (L M S)
WEEKDAYS

P.M.
9.15 Edinburgh, Perth, Aberdeen, Inverness.

9.30 Dumfries, Kilmarnock and Glasgow (St. Enoch).

SUNDAYS

P.M.
9.15 Edinburgh, Perth, Aberdeen, Inverness.

9.30 Dumfries, Kilmarnock and Glasgow (St. Enoch).

With a return ticket to Scotland, you now have the choice of travelling back by the East Coast, West Coast, or Midland routes, with break of journey at any station. PENNY A MILE SUMMER TICKETS are issued every day (first class only two thirds higher) for return any time within one month—break your journey at any station. Ask at any L·N·E·R or L M S Station or Office for Pocket Timetables and Programme of Circular Tours.

IT'S QUICKER BY RAIL

LONDON MIDLAND & SCOTTISH RAILWAY
LONDON & NORTH EASTERN RAILWAY

Railway advertisement (1934)

game; to ground which seems occasionally barren, and which it needs a fine instructed eye to traverse scientifically, and thereof to detect the latent riches. Fear and hope are the deities of the moors, else would they lose their witchcraft. A gentleman ought not to shoot like a gamekeeper, any more than at billiards to play like a marker . . .

Not only did many Guns shoot surprisingly large bags over dogs, but also they would take themselves away to the moors for much of August, sometimes staying on well into September, going out day after day with insatiable appetites for so-called respectable bags. Even when fashion forced them into the butts, the more hardened campaigners continued dogged dogging on by-days.

Today, of course, such opportunities are rare because most moors managed to provide high densities of grouse are geared up to driven sport in order to maximise income. Even if a sympathetic owner did allow frequent dogging he would run the risk of excessive disturbance spoiling his driven days. In the old days grouse-shooters worked with dogs because there was no other way. Now there is a choice, yet dogging remains popular beyond the extent expected through price comparison with driven days. Surely that is proof of the more leisured activity's great attraction and the ever-increasing number of true sports walking tall on our upland wilderness.

Crating birds ready for the gamedealer

12

For the Greater Good

*Wildlife, conservationists, ramblers and the general public
owe much to the custodial attitude of grouse-shooters*

For two centuries only sport tempered the activities of those who would have ravaged our uplands. Without the interest and action of many thousands of grouse-shooters we would have lost countless acres of precious habitat to the god of economics. Admittedly this is fortuitous, because even the grouse-shooters acted largely out of self-interest, but there is no denying that it is they alone who have preserved this last bastion of wilderness for an ever-increasing cross-section of society to enjoy. Now all our leading conservation organisations – both governmental and private – recognise the benefits of positive moorland management by grouse-shooters and, even though some object to shooting on principle, publicly declare their support. The heather-dominated uplands are regarded as Britain's last remaining largely undeveloped wildlife habitat, containing an animal community of international importance.

A good example of shooter-conservationist co-operation comes in the distinctive shape of TV star and leading conservationist David Bellamy, who in 1989 agreed to become patron of the Moorland Gamekeepers' Association even though he does not shoot. In an important article in *Shooting Times*, he said:

> I rejoice in the fact that people can play a part in the economy of a large area of exhilarating landscape, in which no massive application of pesticides need ever be used. I will never join you at the butts, but I will continue to fight alongside you in the protection of our upland heritage. We are both engaged in the same business: the most important business of all, conservation.

It is fair to say that grouse-shooters have bought time for mankind. Through centuries without any clear concept of nature conservation and very little appreciation of landscape, they stood alone in warding off the encroachment of so-called development. Now society is concerned with values other than economic and the era of green awareness has dawned just in time to put weight behind the work of moor-owners. Much heather continues to be lost – about 1–4 per cent per annum – but from now on those who are only concerned with their bank balance will have to fight for every acre. And at the same time the quality of remaining heather-moorland habitat should generally improve, enhancing its holding capacity for innumerable species of plants, birds, mammals, reptiles, amphibians and insects as we reap the benefits of new scientific research.

Some people might argue that we would be better off without some 1,600,000ha (4 million acres) of grouse moor because then, even allowing for increased development, we would have a greater variety of habitats, including scrub and mature woodland, as existed before the hills were settled. However, today these other types of habitat are relatively unimportant because they also exist at lower altitudes. In addition, there are great advantages in having very large areas of habitat rather than mere oases dotted across the land. Species within small reserves are especially vulnerable in that it is difficult for them to maintain viable breeding populations in the face of disaster such as a major fire or pollution incident. The larger the reserve or area of single habitat, the easier it is for a species to recolonise lost ground. This is not such a problem with birds, which are generally more mobile, but with plants and other groups of animal local confinement can spell disaster or even extinction, as has happened with three British species of dragonfly in the last thirty years.

Inevitably, it is birds which receive the greatest attention in any habitat debate because they are generally the most obvious and beautiful creatures coming to notice and the country is blessed with several million birdwatchers. As these enthusiasts have become more mobile they have become increasingly interested in visiting wild places such as the heather moorlands and have been pleasantly surprised by what they have found. This is just as well because more than 90 per cent of heather moorland remains in the hands of sporting estates, which have traditionally maintained this precious habitat through careful management, especially controlled burning and grazing.

Although professional ornithologists and most serious birdwatchers are familiar with reality, there are, unfortunately, many nature enthusiasts for whom a little learning truly is a dangerous thing. For example, they read the occasional popular newspaper report headlined, say, 'Moorland gamekeeper poisons birds of prey' and immediately jump to the conclusion that this is the norm. The truth is that indiscriminate poisoning is rare nowadays because most modern gamekeepers are better educated and enjoy the sight of eagle and falcon as much as any man. No one is pretending that this diabolical killing is not continuing, but it really is only a tiny minority of selfish people concerned and it is more likely to be a hill farmer trying to protect his lambs from foxes than an old keeper baiting crows. Hopefully, better education should soon see an end to this altogether, but in the meantime moor-owners and managers should ensure that every employee is thoroughly familiar with the law. Any transgression should lead to the miscreant's instant dismissal because no amount of sport is worth the life of even one raptor.

Of all the birds, it is the raptors or birds of prey which generate greatest interest in the grouse-moor habitat. In the old days anything with a hooked beak was shot on sight whether or not it was a significant predator of grouse. Today they are all protected, though some misguided individuals would like to be able to control hen harriers, pointing to the species' recent slight increase but not realising that it was primarily persecution by sporting estates which decimated the population in the first place.

At the beginning of this century the hen harrier's British range was virtually confined to the Outer Hebrides and Orkney, with small numbers in Ireland, all areas with few or no large sporting estates. Later, especially during World War II, the number of keepers gradually diminished, so there was less direct persecution and

A Game Conservancy one-day course on grouse management at Leadhills (The Game Conservancy)

decreased heather-burning led to an increase in the amount of tall, rank heather in which hen harriers like to nest. Recolonisation has also been aided by afforestation of many moors because the birds can breed unmolested in the plantations. Today the relative seclusion afforded by sporting estates remains very important in providing a substantial nucleus of breeding and roosting habitat, though in winter many birds gravitate towards lower farmland, marshland and conifer plantations.

Similarly, there is no denying that the decline of the golden eagle was partly due to persecution by gamekeepers, who maintained that, apart from direct predation on grouse, the presence of an eagle might spoil a drive. Fortunately, the golden eagle has made a steady recovery in recent decades, largely through removal of harmful chemicals from sheep dips. Some persecution continues, but it is largely unwarranted as the eagles merely remove a fraction of the cullable grouse surplus and inevitably concentrate on weaker, slower, diseased birds. In any case, recent studies of eagle diet have shown that sheep and deer carrion is more important, especially in winter. Eagles are more at risk from egg-collectors and tourists, as well as inquisitive birdwatchers, and the value of the sporting estate lies chiefly in providing relative seclusion for the eyries. Without keepers and stalkers there would be no one present to warden these vast, remote areas and all other birds of prey would suffer along with the golden eagle.

The peregrine falcon, too, has a similar story. Once unduly persecuted by shooters, it now enjoys the sanctuary provided by the great grouse-shooting estates, where many of its craggy nest-sites enjoy substantial privacy. Many keepers and moor-owners delight in the remarkable hunting skills of these birds and view their presence with great pride and interest. Shooters' remarkable observations of peregrines are many and varied. For example, in the 1989 season, while waiting on a rock for a drive to start, a Gun in Cumbria was surprised when a grouse crashed into his leg and rolled over a few times. The indignant bird cackled, got up and flew away as the man in the next butt pointed skywards towards a peregrine. He explained that the falcon had stooped on the grouse and knocked it down onto the Gun below. On seeing the men the peregrine broke off.

Buzzards, too, forage widely over open moorland, though their chief prey is rodents and birds much smaller than the grouse and their preferred habitat is mixed. The carrion available on grouse moors is important for buzzards when deep snow affords small mammals some protection.

Much rarer, and one of the greatest treasures of the grouse-moor, is that dashing little falcon, the merlin. RSPB head of research Dr Colin Bibby made a special study of the species, which has declined to about six hundred pairs in Britain. He has stated

Beaters must be very fit, and often include students

that the good places for merlins 'coincide very closely with the best places for grouse on the dry heather moors from the eastern Highlands to the Pennines.' Their main prey is small birds. In Wales, Dr Bibby found that in many areas merlins had lost their preferred habitat as heather moorland had been allowed to go to grass through heavy grazing or had been afforested. 'The pairs with a greater abundance of heather moorland bred more successfully than those in areas with more grassy sheep-walks.'

Very recently, British merlins have taken to nesting in conifer plantations, as they do more commonly abroad. However, in Britain over 75 per cent of the population still nests on the ground – *only on grouse-moors*. Just why they took to this artificially maintained habitat with such success remains a mystery. But whatever the reason, we do know that the variety of heather stages generated by systematic muirburn is important to the merlin in providing both suitable nest-sites and food. Furthermore, the correlation with good moor management is exemplified by the fact that where keepering has declined and the fox population has been allowed to increase (especially in mixed sheep and forestry landscapes) the merlin population has generally declined.

Also among birds of prey to make use of our grouse-moors are the beautiful gyrfalcon, the rarest of all winter visitors to Britain, and the equally handsome snowy owl, among the most tenuously established of our breeding species. These large raptors are drawn to the wildest parts of sporting estates in Scotland and the northern isles because the habitat there is not unlike their haunts in the tundra, and grouse is certainly on the menu of most gyrfalcons. Much commoner, and more familar to grouse-shooters, is the short-eared owl, which often hunts by day as well as in the twilight. It appears to be dependent on substantial tracts of open country well away from excessive human disturbance, and where its rodent prey is abundant. Such ideal conditions are commonly found on the sporting estates of upland Britain, especially where patches of well-managed heather are interspersed with areas of rough grazing, young forestry and marsh. In winter many of the owls which breed on moorland move to inland and coastal marshes. Numbers have increased considerably this century due to more sympathetic keepering and the spread of forestry.

Among the many species which benefit from the rough, relatively unspoilt areas which often surround grouse-moors, is the barn owl. In the past such places were fairly insignificant, holding relatively few birds because the species is at its worldwide northern limit in Britain. Today, however, such pockets of suitable habitat are increasingly important as the barn owl continues its alarming decline.

Many species of wader are also very dependent on heather moorland, both for breeding and roosting. Indeed, the golden plover is often regarded as an indicator of the ecological quality of moorland and in some regions, such as the North York Moors, it almost always nests on open ground where the heather has been burned recently by gamekeepers. In Britain the golden plover nests only on the uplands and moorlands of the north and west, where it has lost some ground this century to afforestation, which makes remaining moorland even more important. Along with the red grouse, the golden plover reflects more closely than any other bird species the distribution of moorland, bog and rough grazing in the north and west.

Other common waders which make extensive use of moorland for breeding, feeding and roosting are the curlew, common snipe, oystercatcher, lapwing, common sandpiper, redshank and dunlin. For some of these birds, upland sites have become increasingly important as lowland alternatives have disappeared through drainage, ploughing and other development. Ostensibly suitable lowland sites are often spoilt by excessive disturbance. Ideal conditions are provided by uplands with dry breeding-sites adjacent to streams, bogs and rough grazing for feeding, all commonly found on and about sporting estates.

Some of our rarer waders, too, owe much to the protection of northern estates. Though confined to mountain-top sites in Britain, the dotterel, whose population is generally less than a hundred pairs, enjoys the seclusion provided by surrounding moorlands, which act as an important buffer zone, shielding such vulnerable species from tourists, over-zealous birdwatchers and egg-collectors. Similarly, the whimbrel (under 200 pairs) and the greenshank (400–750 pairs) confine their nesting to the moors and wilds of the far north.

Northern moors are also important in assisting the colonisation of Britain by species whose main range is to the north and east, on the tundra. For example, the Temminck's stint has successfully fledged a small number of broods in Scotland and Yorkshire in recent years. The snow bunting is a very rare breeder confined to the most remote mountain tops, but larger numbers of visitors sometimes feed on the heather moors and rough grasslands.

More common songbirds which make extensive use of grouse-moors and their environs are the meadow pipit, skylark, wheatear and whinchat, all very familiar birds. Another great prize is that beautiful blackbird with a white bib, the ring ouzel, whose distribution closely follows that of high ground throughout most of the British Isles. It favours rock ledges for nesting and, although most sites are natural, many are on the stone walls and buildings commonly found on grouse-moors. Some even nest on the butts. Other common sites are on grass and heather slopes. The twite, too, is very dependent on heather moorland for breeding.

Three species of gamebird also owe much to custodians of the red grouse. Although they require rather different habitat, overlapping only to a limited extent, the black grouse, capercaillie and ptarmigan are jealously protected by northern sportsmen. Proprietors of moors and visiting sportsmen are often equally interested in shooting these birds where viable populations exist and they are concentrated on and around the estates whose main concern is the red grouse.

Although mostly confined to the high tops, the ptarmigan may be shot alongside the red grouse on favoured hills. The black grouse is often encountered when the more scrubby areas of the grouse moor are walked-up, but it is very difficult to drive. Now that it has lost most of its southern range its northern stronghold has assumed a new importance, though even there it remains under great pressure. The capercaillie, the largest member of the grouse family, is also struggling in Britain, being confined almost entirely to east-central Scotland. Although it is primarily a woodland bird, it, too, is indebted to sporting interests. Indeed, it was sportsmen who were responsible for its reintroduction and spread after the large-scale felling of natural pine forests brought about its British extinction at the end of the eighteenth century.

All-terrain vehicles are invaluable on the moor

An excellent example of the variety of birds which are attracted by a well-managed grouse-moor is that provided by Sir Anthony Milbank and his keeper Alan Edwards (secretary of the Moorland Gamekeepers' Association) at their adjoining Barningham (Durham) and Holgate (Yorkshire) moors. In 1988 Sir Anthony won the premier Joseph Nickerson Heather Improvement Foundation Award in recognition of 'endeavour calculated to strengthen the viability of rural communities in the heather uplands by the effective management and integration of sheep- and grouse-farming enterprises.' As a farmer and shooter he has succeeded in juggling many interests, but his achievement as a conservationist is even more remarkable in that about fifteen species of bird regularly nest on his land. These include four or five pairs of ring ouzel, dippers, redshank, oystercatchers, mallard, teal, merlin, short-eared owl, snipe, golden plover, curlew and peewit. 'And carrion crows have tried, but failed,' Sir Anthony told me with a chuckle. Before Sir Anthony took over in 1979, the heather had been under-burnt and the greater part of the moor consisted of over-aged, though still vigorous, heather, but now the regeneration programme is well advanced on this moor where much of the BBC's widely acclaimed film 'A Passion for Grouse' was filmed.

There is one bird, however, which is not generally welcome in the uplands. That is the crow, and it is as much a pest in its grey-and-black form (the hooded crow) as it is in all black (the carrion crow). Both phases are found on grouse-moors, but the hooded predominates in Ireland and north-west Scotland. They are extremely common in upland areas, where they find a major source of food in sheep carrion. However, they also take grouse eggs and chicks in substantial numbers so the grouse keepers must control them as much as possible. This also benefits many of the other species of upland bird mentioned above because the crow also takes their eggs and young. Crow and fox control by moorland gamekeepers makes an enormous contribution to nature conservation in Britain. Man created the conditions which allowed the crow to proliferate and now he must not shirk his responsibility in culling this pest. EEC moves to introduce a close season for crow and magpie from 1 February to 1 September would be disastrous because that is precisely the period when these predators cause maximum damage to grouse stocks and other wildlife.

When it comes to mammals there are two species which have made major gains through moorland management for sport. The blue or mountain hare is extremely common on grouse-moors, where surprisingly few are shot and its diet is not a cause for concern. However, the size of the Scottish deer population has more than trebled since the severe winter of 1946–7 and has aggravated the problem of over-grazing by sheep. Another mammal causing widespread concern is the mink, which has recently colonised much of the country and takes grouse along with many other species. Gamekeepers must control it rigorously.

Less obvious is how many species of insect and other invertebrates benefit through grouse-moor preservation and management. Butterflies, moths and dragonflies abound on many sporting estates and some of them are so specialised they would be hard-pressed to make a living elsewhere. These include the beautiful emperor moth, whose caterpillars feed mostly on heather, and the rare chequered skipper butterfly, which survives only near the Great Glen in Scotland and depends on grazing to maintain a suitable grassy habitat. The large heath butterfly is confined to the uplands and is commonly seen on heather moorlands, especially those with wet areas supporting rich growths of cotton-grass, sedges and fescues – all food plants for its caterpillar. On sunny days the Scotch argus will be seen dancing about the moors, but only higher estates attract the small mountain ringlet, one of Britain's true alpine butterflies, now largely confined to western Scotland and the Lake District. Many of the more widespread butterflies and moths are found at particularly high densities on grouse-moors.

The Duke of Roxburghe and his headkeeper Jimmy Nairn at Byrecleugh

ON THE MOORS

COMPLETE

A GOOD LUNCH

WITH

DEWAR'S

The Famous "White Label"

The blue aeshna dragonfly is found only in Scotland and northern England, and the Highland sympetrum dragonfly is confined to western Scotland and parts of Ireland, wet moors being favoured habitat for both species. Drier moors attract large numbers of bees, heather honey being a great favourite with many people. Less welcome, of course, is the heather beetle, which occasionally causes damage of economic importance when its grubs eat the young leaves and bark at the tips of the shoots, the very parts which are most nutritious for the grouse. Unfortunately there is little that can be done about it because the beetles hibernate underground during the heather-burning season. However, a parasitic wasp accounts for many beetles in years of abundance.

Reptiles and amphibians, too, are generally common on grouse-moors, sometimes being surprisingly abundant in relatively dry places as well as in bogs and near ponds and streams. Adders are particularly numerous on moors as they are specially fond of open areas where it is easy to bask in the sunshine and catch species such as mice and voles which are abundant. Common lizards also like the moors for their sunbathing potential and wealth of prey, notably spiders. Slow-worms, too, favour the sunny situations, especially on damp moors where slugs abound.

This great wealth of animal life is well supported by a fascinating flora of over six hundred species – many of them scarce or very local – which have made the moors their home. As every game-shooter knows, grouseland is not only carpeted with heather; it is a mosaic of many different habitats and micro-climates, each attracting its specialist plants such as bilberry, sundew, sphagnum moss, cotton-grass, bog rosemary, bog sedge, cloudberry, horsetail, brown orchid and butterwort.

With such a rich diversity of animal and plant life dependent on the grouse-moor habitat it is easy to see why conservationists are eager for planned moor management to continue. In particular, a programme of systematic heather-burning is essential to provide the variety of cover necessary to attract many species other than the red grouse at different stages of their lives. Far from being an apparent act of vandalism in the eyes of the casual observer, heather-burning is the saviour of the entire moorland ecosystem. The best method is to burn the heather in strips. Their length is unimportant, but they should not be more than about 30m (33yd) wide because grouse feeding on short heather like to have the safety of longer growth nearby. Similarly, hedgerows and thin strips of woodland or small copses are better for pheasants than huge, unbroken woods. The closeness of cover is specially important for hen grouse with broods which have little or no experience of predators.

A skilled keeper aims to provide heather at three basic heights: up to about 20cm (8in) for sunning and low enough for chicks to feed easily on the nutritious tips; about 45cm (18in) high for nesting cover; and 60cm (24in) high for escape cover and sheltering from severe weather. At the same time he will try to provide patches of each height within small areas so that each pair of grouse have all their requirements within a territory. Because heather grows at widely varying altitudes and in very different climates around the country, its rate of growth varies too, and the burning cycle must

Dewar's advertisement, 1938

be altered accordingly. Whereas many English moors get by on a 10/15-year rotation (ie between a tenth and a fifteenth of the moor is burnt each year), a 30/50-year cycle may suffice in northern Scotland. The plan must also take into account grazing pressure caused by sheep and deer. Incidentally, the latter also benefit from rotational burning because they, too, prefer the tender young leaves and stems to the chewy and less nutritious, old, woody growth.

Muirburn is strictly controlled by law and must stop before the local season for ground-nesting birds begins. In England and Wales it is allowed from 1 November to 31 March, and in Scotland 1 October to 15 April. However, if written permission is obtained from the Ministry of Agriculture (DAFS in Scotland) the burning season may be extended to 30 April or, on ground above 460m (1,500ft) in Scotland, to 15 May. It is vital that heather-burners are alert to early breeding of ground-nesting birds, remembering that commencement of laying will vary with altitude, latitude and longitude, and the mildness of the year. The law provides only guidelines. Even though a season might provide only a few sufficiently dry days with just the right amount of wind, burning should never commence if the breeding of any bird is threatened. How could a grouse-shooter stand easy in his butt knowing that he had cremated the brood or clutch of some rarity?

The beaters put another grouse up

Setting fire to the heather is easy, but controlling the burn is both tiring and exacting, and there is never enough help to hand. The fire must be slow and steady enough to remove all the old growth and debris, leaving a fine ash to enrich the soil, but not so hot the ground is scorched and the roots retarded or even burnt out if the blanket peat catches fire. Apart from destroying wildlife, plants and valuable grazing, ill-considered burning can alter the physical structure, chemical composition and hydrology of the soil as well as mar the appearance of the landscape. No one should commence heather burning without obtaining a copy of the *Heather and Grass Burning Code* from the local office of the Ministry of Agriculture Fisheries and Food. Detailed advice on formulating a long-term management programme is available from the Game Conservancy, whose field advisors will visit a moor for a modest fee.

As well as providing a haven for wildlife, good grouse-moor management protects and enhances a magnificent landscape in which man likes to wander to refresh his world-weary spirit. The seemingly endless moors and mountains offer peace to tourists and invigorating challenges to ramblers and rock-climbers. Sadly, now that this last vestige of wilderness is firmly on the map the weight of human numbers is posing many problems and the question of public access is not going to disappear.

Understandably, hill walkers, championed by the Ramblers' Association, have always worked 'for the right to roam freely over uncultivated mountain and moorland', including grouse-moors. The RA has been influential in helping to secure access agreements for a number of moors, particularly in the Peak District, which is close to significant centres of human population. At the moment they are actively campaigning for 'public access to be given to grouse-moor commons' and 'do not accept that ramblers on these moors have a detrimental effect on the shooting there'. Sadly, many of these ramblers are not concerned whether or not the land is in private ownership, is a Site of Special Scientific Interest or even a nature reserve. Their determination to trample over everything and everybody dominates their thinking.

Fortunately, there is substantial middle ground which must be explored and the moderates allowed to draft compromise. Contrary to the image often portrayed in the popular press, most moor-owners are not super-rich, gun-toting idiots who immediately set upon anyone who sets foot on their precious acres. Almost to a man, they believe that *controlled* access is the answer, and they have the powerful conservation lobby behind them. Quite apart from the relatively minor problems of litter and erosion of footpaths, there are the major worries of uncontrolled fires caused by camp fires and cigarette ends, and disturbance and killing of both grouse and wildlife, especially by dogs not on leads. In a few hours, a major conflagration can destroy hundreds of acres of precious habitat which it has taken many years to create, at the same time killing both plants and wildlife, some of which may already be rare. Sensitive birds may be so stressed they fail in their breeding, perhaps deserting their nests or returning to find eggs or chicks taken by predators. The rarer the species, the more acute the problem.

Disturbance of actual shooting days is also a very serious problem. A party of Guns robbed of a successful drive because some inconsiderate fool in a bright orange anorak walks over the horizon is obviously going to want compensation. And when they are paying thousands of pounds for their sport the loss to the estate is very substantial indeed. Moors with continuing problems are going to find it very difficult to attract a steady stream of paying guests and as a result may have to curtail their management programmes. Then the wildlife will suffer along with the local economy and the ramblers themselves will lose the charm and character of the heather-moor landscape in which they revel.

Such problems are being addressed by the Moorland Association, whose members, both public and private landowners, rallied together when the Government asked the Countryside Commission to look into stage two legislation concerning common land. The Countryside Commission formed the Common Land Forum, which produced wide-ranging recommendations for the Government, one of which was the uproarious idea that there should be unrestricted public access on common land. Moorland Association member Lord Peel, also chairman of the Game Conservancy's North of England Grouse Research Project, commented:

> Ministers must be prevented from allowing this crazy idea of allowing the public to walk wherever they want to. It must be understood that it is impossible to manage the land if you are unable to manage people. I believe we have got to the stage where more control of the public, not less, is needed.

Many grouse-moor owners shoot some beats only a couple of times a year, yet must maintain the land for the other 363 days. Why should they pay huge sums for others to receive most of the benefits? Surely controlled access that does not interfere with the complex interrelationship of conservation, sport and landscape is the only way ahead. And at the same time all those who wish to enjoy a moor should pay towards its upkeep. Perhaps the answer is to sell permits which specify exactly when, where, how often and why people may visit. Some financial compensation is already contained within a few agreements, such as those within the Peak District National Park, where owners receive a very small amount per acre for 'overall diminution due to public access'.

Grouse-shooters and moor-owners certainly have many problems to sort out if sport is to continue on its current scale into the next century. Quite apart from age-old problems such as balancing the books, competing land uses and 'antis', there is always some new problem lurking on the horizon. In one area it might be low-flying aircraft, in another air pollution killing off the lichens and mosses which start the binding and regenerating process where heather has been lost. And yet there is no widespread apathy. On the contrary, there is great optimism among grouse-shooters generally and this is leading to plenty of positive action. Of special note is the increasing interest in heather regeneration, which is now reasonably well supported by a system of Government grants because at long last heather is rightly recognised as a crop, benefitting both graziers and sportsmen. Much of the impetus has come from the Joseph Nickerson Heather Improvement Foundation, which was formed in 1985.

Loss of heather has been insidious and widespread throughout this century. Over 40 per cent, 800,000ha (2 million acres), of Britain's heather moorland has

FOR THE MOORS

To get "the best" out of the moors it is well to be prepared for all weathers, and have a care that the clothing to be worn is inconspicuous in the Butts and especially when walking up, when you will see grouse that are swinging back over the line avoiding conspicuous guns.

BURBERRY SHOOTING SUIT

The best possible camouflage is Gamefeather Tweeds which are woven in the colours and on the principles of the plumage of game birds. These beautiful suitings are available in fine Saxonies as well as Scotch Cheviots. They provide perfect freedom. Pivot sleeves, a Burberry invention, release arms and shoulders from all sense of restraint.

THE BURBERRY

The Burberry is extremely light in weight, perfectly weatherproof, never heating on the mildest days, and its fine texture prevents cold wind penetration. Its colour completely camouflages the wearer.

Burberrys advertisement (1939)

Illustrations, patterns and prices on mention of "Game and Gun."

BURBERRYS HAYMARKET LTD. LONDON, S.W.1

disappeared since World War II. Today only 34,000ha (85,000 acres) of heather are left in the whole of Wales, a mere 1,200ha (3,000 acres) remain on Dartmoor, and on the North York Moors over 77 sq km (30 sq miles) have gone in the last forty years, chiefly through afforestation. Cumbria has lost 70 per cent of its heather since the last war. However, regression in England overall is put at 22 per cent whereas Scotland's is said to be around 37 per cent. Today much of the lost ground is occupied by poor-quality 'white' grasses, the result of poor burning and grazing practices. Forestry now covers some 20 per cent of British uplands, while bracken and moorland grasses occupy 40 per cent, leaving just 40 per cent dominated by heather.

The situation in Scotland seems to be getting worse compared with England, where keeper density is 30 per cent higher. More importantly, English keepers generally spend more of their time on grouse-related work than their Scottish colleagues do (55 per cent as opposed to 41 per cent). This is specially important in predator control, and therefore it is not surprising that, taken together, English moors produce over two and a half times as many grouse per unit of moorland on a ten-year average. Indeed, although their heather cover is decreasing, studies indicate that the yield of birds per unit of heather is increasing. Despite more heavily stocked moors, more bracken, less subsidy and more common land, English moors still manage a net farm-plus-shooting income four and a half times greater than that in Scotland, where the Less Favoured Area (LFA) subsidies substantially exceed the net farm income.

Among the most serious threats to remaining heather is the rapid spread of bracken, which not only displaces the heather but also is poisonous to farm stock, harbours disease which affects both grouse and sheep and impoverishes the habitat for many species.

When companies buy up cheap hill land and plant it with a monoculture of conifers they not only further reduce the area of heather but also increase sanctuary for predators which take ground-nesting birds, including grouse. These tax-cut forestry people mostly have no concern for the uplands generally and are faceless investors who live far away.

Equally disastrous is over-grazing, largely due to changes in traditional shepherding practices. With fewer shepherds on the moor, greater concentrations of sheep near winter foddering points and uneven dispersal of sheep, the heather has been eaten and trampled right out in many areas and replaced by coarse grasses. Judicious use of feed blocks can alleviate the problem in spreading the load across wider areas.

Although heather regeneration is sometimes possible through the simple measure of fencing out sheep and deer, this is not always acceptable on financial grounds. Where the heather has been largely eradicated a substantial management input is necessary, involving spraying invasive vegetation, preparing the ground and reseeding – a costly exercise. However, while the new conservation grants will benefit small areas, they will not arrest general decline of heather moorland. The only answer would appear to be reducing the pressure of winter grazing through restructuring the current support system. Perhaps the time will come when sheep farmers will have to be subsidised to under-graze the moors.

Managed sensibly, grouse and sheep can enjoy harmonious coexistence on heather moorland. Indeed, when they graze evenly over a moor sheep are actually beneficial to heather and grouse in promoting nutritious new growth. However, the doubling of the national flock since 1947 cannot be tolerated, any more than profit-hungry investors can be allowed to destroy the nation's rich heritage of upland wildlife and landscape through indiscriminate afforestation. At the same time ways should be sought to discourage landowners from putting even more heather moorland under the plough to create pasture.

Although the nation's flock is about the size it was a century ago, there is less moorland suitable for the sheep to graze on now because so much has been lost to forestry, bracken etc. The alarming and steady encroachment of bracken is put at 2.8 per cent per annum for the British Isles, even higher than afforestation – estimated at 2.75 per cent – and loss to urban development put at 2.1 per cent. Perhaps the worst aspect of bracken spread is that it provides relatively poor wildlife habitat: only 15 species of bird generally breed in it, compared with 33 species in heather and 25 on acidic grasslands. Even worse is the fact that some nationally important species such as the hen harrier and greenshank avoid it entirely.

To compound the problem, over the last century, and especially since the introduction of support farming in 1947, lowland sheep farming has declined as flocks have gravitated towards the uplands. Heather is by far the most important of the few evergreens available on moorlands and as it usually remains exposed in light snow cover it is a crucial part of the hill sheep's autumn and winter diet. Because of its availability over 80 per cent of sheep are kept on English and Scottish moors in winter.

This whole question of competition between grouse and grazing animals became the focus of a special Reconciliation Project set up in 1984 and scheduled to last ten years. Surely one of its priorities must be to encourage a more rigorous hind cull in Scotland. One way would be to remove the sporting rates which are levied on hind shooting. The abolition of all sporting rates in Scotland would give grouse-shooting a tremendous boost. Moors in England and Wales are free of this considerable burden so it is little wonder that Scottish moors are generally less cost-effective. It is bad enough that a moor should suffer declining grouse stocks, but to add insult to injury Scottish rates are based on an earlier five-year assessment. So when the inevitable local grouse population crash comes along on a cyclical basis a moor may well find that it is assessed on ten times as many grouse as it now has. Abolition of this anomaly would encourage hard-pressed landowners to take on more gamekeepers, whose scarcity is at the root of many problems, and this would increase grouse stocks.

Fortunately, the demand for grouse-shooting continues to be quite staggering. For example, in 1989 the best moors received up to £75 plus VAT per brace and £50–60 was common. In comparison, the cream of pheasant shoots took just £22 per bird and the majority of excellent estates had to be content with £14–16, all plus VAT. In addition, there is a fear that the price of pheasant shooting may have peaked whereas that for grouse appears to have no ceiling. It is a fantastic sport and everyone who tries it wants to come back time and time again.

Overleaf: *Muirburn (The Game Conservancy)*

Much of this stimulus comes from overseas, and in recent years we have even seen Japanese in the butts alongside a steady stream of Americans and visitors from just about every country in Europe. Many of these foreigners not only buy single days but also keenly rent moors for entire seasons. Some have even bought entire estates primarily for the sport offered, and if that sport is top-notch it adds very considerably to the estate agent's asking price. Some new purchasers are prepared to invest heavily in their acquisitions and this is just the kind of boost the sport needs.

Another noticeable development is the number of younger people filling the butts, many of them not having entered the sport before adulthood. Some of them are business executives who cut their teeth on a company clayshoot, laid on as a kind of perk for high-achievers or important customers. The good news is that many of them are so impressed they take to the sport for life. The bad news is that not all of them receive the service they deserve from commercial operators. No matter who the customer is or what his knowledge of game-shooting may be, he must be offered quality at every level. The market is changing rapidly. No longer is it dependent on the plutocrat who could afford to spend four or five weeks on the moor without interruption. Today's typical paying customer lives life in the fast lane and he will think no more of jetting up to the Highlands for a day's sport than he will of buying tickets for the ballet or Centre Court at Wimbledon. Give him the service he expects and he will come back with the money to secure the future of this unequalled sport.

Sufficient funding is necessary for sound management based on *facts*, and the managers must shoot only to the level of each year's production. Some commercial shoots must be more honest with bag predictions. Sadly, there are a few lazy moor-owners and managers who take a lot and give little, hoping that researchers will produce a magic cure-all. They won't, as evidenced by the continuing decline of the grey partridge despite decades of research. Yes, we have the concept of conservation headlands, but the combined efforts of the few managers putting the theory into practice are a drop in the ocean. Whether it's partridges or grouse, *consistent* good management of the habitat and *strict* control of man's activities within and without the sporting field are the main answers. Truly pioneering research is always welcome but we must guard against squandering of resources through duplication of effort.

Sound management based on proven traditional methods is only a beginning. We must not allow ourselves to be side-tracked so often in pursuit of solutions to relatively minor issues when the core problem of habitat loss looms large. For such a small island we really do have too many people chasing too many diverse and often opposing interests. Surely it is time for a far-sighted and co-ordinated national countryside policy with due consideration for wildlife, landscape and leisure activities such as shooting, hiking and birdwatching. Free-market forces have held the floor for too long and it is only through sheer luck and the shooting world's love of the glorious grouse that we still have so much unspoilt moorland to enjoy. If upland-owners are expected to continue as guardians of Britain's last great wilderness and public playground then ways must be found to give them the nation's financial as well as moral support. Those who dare to enter grouseland without contributing to its welfare should heed the advice of the grouse itself and *go-back, go-back*.

Bibliography

Alken, Henry. *The National Sports of Great Britain* (1821)

Arnold, Edwin, Lester. *Bird Life in England* (1887)

Ascham, Roger. *Toxophilus, the Schole of Shooting conteyned in two Bookes* (1545)

Bloome, Richard. *The Gentleman's Recreation* (1686)

Carlisle, Gordon. *Grouse and Gun* (Stanley Paul, 1983)

Clement, Lewis. *Shooting Yachting and Sea-fishing Trips* (Chapman and Hall, 1876)

Colquhoun, John. *The Moor and the Loch* (Blackwood, 1840)

Cramp, Stanley (ed). *The Birds of the Western Palearctic* Vol 2 (OUP, 1980)

Craven. *Recreations in Shooting* (Chapman and Hall, 1846)

Daniel, Rev R. B. *Rural Sports* (Longman etc, 1807)

Eden, Ronald. *Going to the Moors* (John Murray, 1979)

Fuller, R. J. *Bird Habitats in Britain* (Poyser, 1982)

Hawker, Col Peter. *Instructions to Young Sportsmen* (1814)

Hopkins, Harry. *The Long Affray* (Secker and Warburg, 1985)

Hudson, Peter. *Red Grouse – The Biology and Management of a Wild Gamebird* (The Game Conservancy, 1986)

Hudson, P., and Rands, M., (editors). *Ecology and Management of Gamebirds* (BSP, 1986)

Johnsgard, Paul. *The Grouse of the World* (Croom Helm, 1983)

Knox, A. E. *Game Birds and Wild Fowl* (John Van Voorst, 1850)

Lack, P., (ed). *The Atlas of Wintering Birds in Britain and Ireland* (Poyser, 1986)

Lovat, Lord (ed). *The Grouse in Health and Disease* (Smith Elder, 1911)

Malcolm, G., and Maxwell, A. *Grouse and Grouse Moors* (A. & C. Black, 1910)

Martin, Brian P. *Sporting Birds of the British Isles* (David & Charles, 1984)

Mather, John. *The Birds of Yorkshire* (Croom Helm, 1986)

McKelvie, Colin. *A Future for Game* (George Allen and Unwin, 1985)

Morris, Rev F. O. *A History of British Birds* (Groombridge, 1851–7)

Oakleigh, T. *The Oakleigh Shooting Code* (James Ridgway, 1837)

Parker, Eric. *Shooting Days* (1918)

Pennant, Thomas. *A Tour in Scotland* (John Monk, 1774)

Sharrock, J. (ed). *The Atlas of Breeding Birds in Britain and Ireland* (Poyser, 1977)

Speedy, Tom. *Sport in the Highlands and Lowlands of Scotland* (William Blackwood, 1884)

Stanford, J. K. *The Twelfth* (Faber and Faber, 1944)

St John, Charles. *A Tour in Sutherland* (John Murray, 1849)

St John, Charles. *Sketches of the Wild Sport and Natural History of the Highlands* (John Murray, 1845)

Tate, Peter. *Birds Men and Books* (Sotheran, 1986)

Thom, Valerie. *Birds in Scotland* (Poyser, 1986)

Thornhill, R. B. *The Shooting Directory* (Longman etc, 1804)

Thornton, Col Thomas. *A Sporting Tour through the Northern Parts of England and Greater Part of the Highlands of Scotland* (1804)

Turner, William. *Avium Praecipuarum Historia* (1554)

Vesey Fitzgerald, Brian. *British Game* (Collins, 1946)

Walsingham, Lord, and Payne-Gallwey, Sir Ralph. *Shooting – Moor and Marsh* (1886)

Watson, A., and Miller, I. *Grouse Management*, Game Conservancy booklet 12 (1976)

Acknowledgements

So many people have added to my knowledge of grouse-shooting over the years it would be impossible to list them all here. However, specifically in connection with this book I must express my gratitude to Lady Mary Biddulph, her son Nicholas and their headkeeper Colin Adamson at the Lammermuirs shoot; the Earl Peel and his headkeeper Brian Burrows at Gunnerside; His Grace The Duke of Roxburghe, his headkeeper Jimmy Nairn and keeper Drew Ainslie at Byrecleugh; His Grace The Duke of Westminster for kindly writing the foreword; Willie Veitch, ex-keeper at Byrecleugh; the editors of *The Field* and *Shooting Times & Country Magazine* for permission to include extracts from their journals; and my editors at David & Charles – Sue Hall and Sarah Widdicombe.

PICTURE CREDITS
All photographs taken by the author except those on pages 12, 91, 127 and 184. Photographs on pages 73, 77 and 87 are reproduced by gracious permission of Her Majesty The Queen, and those on pages 135, 137, 140, 151, 157, 201 and 216–17 by kind permission of the Game Conservancy. The advertisement on page 208 is reproduced by kind permission of Arthur Bell Distillers and that on page 13 by kind permission of Matthew Gloag & Son Ltd. The Tryon Gallery gave their kind permission to reproduce the illustrations on pages 10, 19, 25, 29, 33, 45, 65, 83, 106–7 and 158.

Index

Page numbers in **bold** refer to illustrations